HELLO
AVATAR

HELLO AVATAR

Rise of the Networked Generation

B. Coleman

The MIT Press
Cambridge, Massachusetts
London, England

This book was designed by Katie Andresen.

Library of Congress Cataloging-in-Publication Data
Coleman, Beth.
Hello avatar / B. Coleman.
   p. cm.
Includes bibliographical references and index.
ISBN 978-0-262-01571-4 (hardcover: alk. paper)
ISBN 978-0-262-54989-9 (paperback) 1. Virtual reality—Philosophy.
2. Reality. 3. Avatars (computer graphics)—Psychological aspects. 4. Human
behavior models. 5. Shared virtual environments. 6. Human-computer interaction.
I. Title.
BD331.C565   2011
302.23'1—dc22

                                        2010042676

HOW2

Contents

Foreword

Clay Shirky

I started using the Internet in the early 1990s, when the web was just a gleam in Tim Berners-Lee's eye. One of the things I observed during the explosion of the online landscape at that time was a dramatic shift from the text-only medium it had been for its first twenty years of its life to one that was increasingly visual.

It was easy to extrapolate, from this embrace of the image, that the end-state of networked technologies would be our arrival in "cyberspace" and immersion in "virtual reality," phrases bequeathed to us by science fiction author William Gibson and computer scientist Jaron Lanier, respectively. These phrases described a visual but mediated realm where we could interact with data and, much more important, with one another without regard to our geographic location.

By the late 1990s, the evidence for the spread of virtual reality was everywhere—Mark Pesce had created Virtual Reality Markup Language, a general-purpose tool for building virtual environments, and a variety of companies and technologies like Black Sun (later Blaxxun) and Alpha Worlds sprang up to offer computer-mediated visually

immersive experiences. It was easy to guess that virtual
reality would soon become the principal way for people
to interact with one another online.

And then a funny thing happened—it didn't. The
second great change, not as immediately obvious as the
Internet's visual turn but just as profound, was that the
tools of digital connectivity would become ubiquitous.

Back in the day (around 1994), we had our real friends,
whom we saw at work and in the bar, and we had our
imaginary friends, whom we "saw" online. These two
groups were different because the people we knew in the
real world were mostly not online (and in fact had mostly
not heard of the Internet). Conversely, our online friends
didn't live near us, so we couldn't see them in what we
used to call real life, back when it didn't include digital
communication.

The notion of cyberspace was supported by this social
separation—digital networks were seen as an alternative
to the real world, conceptualized as a place where we
would go when we went online. By the early part of this
decade, though, the real and virtual worlds had begun
to anneal.

The first source of this change was growing ubiquity
of access. In 2000, if you were under thirty, you were,
statistically, online, and if you were under 20, most of the
people you knew were online as well. For this cohort,
digital networks were increasingly an augmentation of
the real world, rather than an alternative to it.

Ubiquity of access was followed by ubiquity of connection. A whole host of technologies, from laptops to wireless networks to pocket-sized computers masquerading
as phones, forced us to give up the notion of connecting
as travel, with the destination being online, a place we
would go. To take advantage of digital communications and
use digital tools to read and write digital traces from our
friends and colleagues, we no longer had to sit in particular chairs in front of computers with special wires in the
back. Instead, we could be periodically connected, in short
bursts, all the time.

For most of us thinking about media, these two notions—of a visually immersive cyberspace and of portable, ubiquitous connectivity—exist as alternate interpretations of contemporary behavior. On the cyberspace side, Second Life and Cyworld and Habbo Hotel are visual environments built around architectural metaphors—rooms in which to socialize or visual scenes of travel as we move to different locations in order to converse with others. These spaces were meant as platforms for thick, immersive experiences that were meant to make the real world fall away by copying enough of its affordances and constraints to provide a partial digital substitute.

On the ubiquity side, we have services like Facebook and Flickr and Foursquare, thin tools that allow us to communicate and to share things with one another but which dispense spatial metaphors in favor of emphasizing the connections and locations of the real world over anything immersive.

These notions have generally been treated as incompatible views—if we think of the network as a cyberspace and ourselves as actors enveloped by it, we will analyze our life with the network in one way; if we think of the network as a light, ubiquitous communications substrate linking real-world actors and actions, we will think of it in an alternate way.

What Beth Coleman proposes to do in *Hello Avatar* is nothing less than reconciling those two visions, providing a means to escape the seeming incommensurability of two competing models. Coleman understands media use is a whole complex of cultural practices that represent not alternate visions but alternate choices, sometimes engaged in rapid succession, or even simultaneously. She presents the use of these tools not as fealty to one or the other metaphor for interpreting our behavior but rather as a whole, organic set of explorations and practices, and she wants to help us understand it that way as well.

The distinction between immersive and lightweight uses of the network was only ever theoretical anyway, happily ignored by the actual users of the technologies. People who play World of Warcraft also send text messages to each other, and many of their communications outside the game world are with people they know in the game world as well. The different forms of communication just represent different ways for the same two people to communicate with one another—the presentation of facets in everyday life.

These alternate tools and practices, assumptions and traces, aren't alternates at all when we take a holistic view of the actors involved. Coleman sets aside competing technological metaphors for participation in these networks and shifts her view (and ours) to center on the human actors who are cheerfully and fruitfully crossbreeding these separate media experiences. Our choice of expressing selfhood in various ways, in a medium with this much fluidity and malleability, means that even when we merely set out to consume mediated experiences, we end up as designers of those experiences—sometimes by embracing that possibility as an alternative to a norm of pure consumption, but often just as a side effect of the ways the tools work and the way we work with them.

Coleman's framing image is of an avatar—a constructed trace, sometimes crafted, sometimes recorded, and often both—that represents us in digital congress. The word "avatar," borrowed from the Hindu idea of the manifestation of a god in a form that can be seen in this world, has been pressed into service to mean a manifestation of a person projected into a digital world.

Coleman describes the myriad ways that the idea of the avatar, of the virtual face by which we know one another in digital environments, is not in fact contained by the most explicitly designed virtual worlds but smears across all our digital relations, operating in any space where we recognize each other by our digital traces. A profile on a social network, a photo we use when messaging one another, a brief bio tied to a YouTube account—all of these things have some aspect of the avatar around them.

By insisting that the idea of the avatar be located not in one particular kind of space, around one particular set of media use, Coleman's signal achievement here is to

insist that the media landscape and our place in it is in fact
as complicated as it seems to be. This in turn allows her
to rehumanize a kind of analysis that has often regarded
our own behavior as something so shaped by the medium
that little regard needs to be taken for individual choice.
The cross-media landscape Coleman writes about, the
"x-media" we increasingly swim in, doesn't just cross from
one kind of medium use to another; it crosses from the real
to the mediated world and back, all the time. Despite the
idea of the avatar as a kind of alternate self, identity isn't
just something we put on and take off like a coat—our roles
online are all informed by our own persistent identities.

By rehumanizing the study of technologically sophis-
ticated media use, Coleman shows that we play every role
with deference to some facet of ourselves, and that when
we play those roles with self-regard but without regard
for others, we get the kind of predictable and negative
outcomes such a platform for narcissism would produce.
This kind of analysis doesn't blame the tool—"The Internet
makes us shouty and mean!"—nor does it blame us—
"Behold the squabbling, anonymous masses, humanity in
a state of nature!"—but rather says that when we interact
with one another in a mediated landscape, we do so with
regard to ourselves and to others as filtered through the
expectations our digital traces create. As Coleman notes,
when we play in the network using an avatar with little
history or future, and with other avatars in the same state,
the results can be dismal, but when we present facets
of ourselves that we invest in, and interact with others so
invested, the results can be astonishing.

Hello Avatar is a human account of the current media
environment, concentrating not just on the human use
of tools but on the human use of human beings, to quote
Coleman quoting pioneering cyberneticist Norbert Wiener.
For such a capacious theoretical vision, *Hello Avatar* is also
remarkably concerned with not just theory but principles
that can be used in design practice.

The tools and practices Coleman describes don't just
relate to utilitarian tool use but to our sense of self and of

society. She offers various principles throughout the book
that can be abstracted from her observations, like this one,
which frames her interview with a virtual cannibal: "Users
may not see a virtual forum as central to their daily life;
this does not mean they will not use it in a satisfying way."
In discussing the affordances of digital spaces, she offers
this design principle: "It is the combination of the avatar
appearance and behavior that makes for the most evocative
results." These observations are there to help us not just
understand these digital environments and experiences
better, but to perform them better, which means becoming
better codesigners of our own experiences.

Acknowledgments

Thank you to Howard Goldkrand, Wendy H. K. Chun,
Hal Abelson, Henry Jenkins, and Stefan Helmreich for
their devoted support of the project. With great generosity
of time and spirit, each one read the manuscript at various
stages of development. I am indebted to the amazing
Katie Andresen for her cunning book design and acid wit—
may the two never be parted. Ashley Linnenbank made
sure the design was properly executed, for which we are
all thankful. I am grateful to the broad community participating in this debate about what is real and how we locate
it across our various networks. Mark Wallace and Ren
Reynolds both played excellent Virgils as I made my way
through the circles of virtual worlds. Clay Shirky, thank you
for your provocations on participatory culture that started
this ball rolling—it's all your fault;-) As I followed my trail
across countries, in Paris and Berlin, Caecilia Tripp, Nico
Guiraud, and Lucian Busse were exemplary hosts. I am
very thankful to Joe Paradiso and Irving Wladawsky-Berger
for their enduring interest and inspiration. Also, a sincere
thank you to Jim Paradis for his faith in my investigation
of networked subjects. My colleagues in the Columbia

University Engendering Archives group provided extremely
helpful feedback on chapters, as did the wonderful
Gabriella Coleman. Postdoctorate researcher Jaroslav
Svelch provided great assistance on the timeline. My
appreciation goes to my editor, Doug Sery, for his early and
sustained enthusiasm, as well as to associate editor
Katie Helke Dokshina and the rest of the MIT Press team.
Additionally, I would like to acknowledge the anonymous
peer reviewers for their insights. During my 2010 research
fellowship at Microsoft Research New England, danah
boyd and the social media research group swooped in at
the end of the process to keep me in good company. And,
finally, thanks to the Global Frequency massive for keeping
things wobbly.

B. Coleman, Spring 2011
Cambridge, Massachusetts

Rise of the
Networked Generation:
An Introduction

```
{
state_entry()
{
llSay(0, "Hello, Avatar!");
}
```

Hello Avatar!

Hello Avatar: Worlds of Agency
The script that begins this introduction, *{llSay(0, "Hello,
Avatar!");}*, prints on the computer screen in human language to say, "Hello Avatar!" It is a tiny piece of code that
uses the Linden Scripting Language (LSL) developed by
Linden Lab for the Second Life virtual world platform.
One of the beauties of this language is that it is designed to
be inclusive. Many people without background in computer
coding can and do write scripts to create the animations
and events they choose to enact on the virtual platform.
As with other forms of user customization or user-created
content, LSL is a tool with which users can dig into the
medium of virtual worlds and create their unique vision—

1. Network theory de-
scribes a set of behav-
iors to which a variety
of systems—technical,
natural, or social—
adhere. Much like the
network behavior it
describes, the literature
on network theory is
expansive, crossing
disciplines and con-
necting a diversity of
thinkers. Among the
key theorists, physicist
Albert-László Barabási
has been instrumental
in defining the math-
ematical properties
of networks, and soci-
ologist Manuel Castells
has helped to develop
a theory of networks in
regard to society.

2. Beth Coleman,
"Race as Technology,"
Camera Obscura 24,
Duke University Press
(Fall 2009): 176–190.

one that others can now see right alongside them in a shared vista of virtual objects.

A collaborative space hosted across computers (such as a virtual world), a mesh of mobile phone calls among a group of friends, a live video stream connecting two people on the Internet, these are all examples of networked media we use to connect with each other across geographical distances and often in real time. At the most basic level, the term network describes a system in which nodes are connected to each other by way of links.[1] In a social network, the nodes would be people. In a biological one, the nodes might be proteins linked to form a metabolic network.

In this book, I argue that what we do with our networks of exchange helps to create the world in which we live. And the question of what we do is one of agency. In the field of game studies, agency is often defined as the player's ability to impact the world in which she is playing. Here, I define agency in a fairly narrow manner: user creation with networked media tools. That definition helps to mind the boundaries of my research even as it continues to resonate with the broader terms of agency. As I have argued in previous work, agency indicates presence, will and movement (the ability to move freely as a being) and is not restricted to individuals but also pertains to systems, i.e., it concerns how beings are subjected in systems of power, ideology, and other networks.[2] Technological agency speaks to the ways that external devices help us navigate the terrain in which we live. In thinking about the position of the networked subject, I see yet another turn in the framing of society and self in which agency itself is the disruptive technology of the pervasive media age. In calling agency a technology, I describe a world in which our reach is extended and amplified in terms of spheres of influence, sites of engagement, and presence to one another.

I see a changing face of real-world engagement affected by the emergence of pervasive media. The scale and scope of this change speaks to a generational shift, in which we create new practices of everyday engagement around a set of real-time, highly visual, and cooperatively shared technologies. With this generation of networked media engagement, I see an end of the virtual and the acceleration of the augmented.

This, then, is the generation I address in this work: the emergent age of mobile, pervasive, networked connectivity. This generation is not defined by demographics since I do not speak exclusively of youth and media use (though, many of the examples I cite and people I have interviewed fit this description). The generational shift I discuss is societal and, as I argue, global as we adjust to the growing phenomenon of pervasive media engagement.

Over the past twenty years, much of the analysis in media studies has focused on the shift from analog to digital production as well as the network culture that has proliferated as a result of this shift. In this book I argue that we have already deeply incorporated network society into our lives and that the important change to understand is the continuum between online and off, i.e., the "X-reality" that traverses the virtual and the real. Recognizing the impact of these changes, it is imperative to understand in concert how media is designed and used. Technology does not determine the subject. Yet, we are not entirely free of cultural constructions, including the technological advances that inform who we are. This book addresses our next steps, for good or ill, in the story of the human use of human beings (to invoke the mathematician Norbert Wiener) and of media as the extension of man (to hail media theorist Marshall McLuhan). It also addresses our next steps, also for good or ill, in the story of accelerated mediation or how we continue to augment our reality. It is an exploration of the technical affordances and cultural values of our experience as networked subjects. I believe we are obliged to think about media from both technical and humanistic perspectives if we are to understand our past and build the future we want.

Hello Avatar focuses on what I call *X-reality*—a continuum of exchanges between virtual and real spaces. In this book I look at the emergence of a pervasive media

3. J. N. Bailenson and J. Blascovich, "Avatars." In *Encyclopedia of Human–Computer Interaction* (Great Barrington, MA: Berkshire Publishing Group, 2004), 64–68.

4. The 3D web or X3D refers to the idea that all of the things in which we engage in two dimensions on the web, such as web pages, very soon will be transformed into immersive space (3D) that can be navigated. The 3D web consortium describes its platform as "the real-time communication of 3D data across all applications and network applications," <http://www.web3d.org/about/overview/>. "Semantic web" is a term established by computer scientist Tim Berners-Lee to describe a metalayer of data or an informational "skin" that would make the Internet as it exists a more efficient and responsive database, <http://www.w3.org/>.

use that defines a world that is no longer either virtual or real but representative of a diversity of network combinations. In the course of this research I have found powerful ways in which we are already mixing realities. As a suite of use and design principles, i.e., technologies and ways of engaging those technologies, X-reality speaks to an extension of agency.

My argument is that it is the avatar's role to aid us in expressing this agency. I mean not only the animated figures moving across the screen but also the gestalt of images, text and multimedia that make up our identities as networked subjects. With his film *Avatar* (2009), Director James Cameron has helped to popularize the concept of other bodies representing a single identity. In regard to networked media, I argue that the meaning of avatar includes the many modes of representation we employ that make up the different roles we play and places we go. My broad definition coincides with the standard definition established by researchers of virtual identity and experience.[3] It also addresses the changing media landscape that we occupy. We find avatars in graphical, real-time, spatial simulation environments such as virtual worlds. In a network society, we also find them in the workings of our daily lives in the form of email missives, video connections, and other digital artifacts.

In the everyday life of the networked subject, what avatar culture and X-reality point to is not a new Internet as some have speculated in discussing a 3D web and a semantic web.[4] Rather, today's emergent use suggests signs of change in network behavior characterized by real-time collaborative networks and an experience of copresence that the text-based and asynchronous online world has barely touched upon in terms of the scale of participation. In my analysis, avatar provides a shorthand for the experience of the networked subject, describing different practices of agency, identity and network capability.

Some of the forums in which we are experimenting with new modes of mediated communication are charmingly goofy. By the summer of 2008, the cartoonish virtual world Habbo (Finland) had 9.5 million unique users walking around looking like 8-bit cartoon characters. On the other side of the spectrum, researchers in fields such as neuroscience, psychology, and military are using avatars and 3D interactive forums for both training and experimental work. Both uses—that of popular culture and scientific study—represent serious forums for critical practice of real-time mediated interactions.

Note on Method

In *Hello Avatar* I explore the culture of mediated communication and not just its technologies. My goal is to combine a discourse of theoretical and applied knowledge relating to the subject at hand. I work to critically engage parallel histories of media technologies, scientific research agendas, and the experiences of media participants themselves to form a more holistic view of a networked generation. The scholarship on virtuality, simulation, and virtual worlds has grown over the past thirty years in parallel with the rise of international personal-computing cultures. I draw on that history for my analysis of the contemporary moment of pervasive media engagement. In addition to my analysis of history, state, and practice, I also conducted field research across multiple sites.

I began my field research on the subject of virtual world engagement in the fall of 2006. Over a two-year period, I traveled in various virtual world platforms, as well as to real-world conferences, industry gatherings, meetups, and all manner of X-reality road stops along the way. I conducted much of my research with the online players of Second Life, Club Penguin, There.com, and Habbo, as well as on the forums that served those communities. These interviews were conducted almost entirely via avatar or other forms of mediated communication such as email and Internet telephony. During the course of my fieldwork, I also interviewed virtual world participants, designers, and companies with whom I met in person at professional conferences and social meetups. The United States, Great Britain, France, and Germany were the primary

5. Christine Hine, ed.,
*Virtual Methods: Issues
in Social Research on
the Internet* (Oxford:
Berg 2005).

sites for such meetings. Over the course of the research
I interviewed several hundred people. However, in writing
I chose to highlight a select group of interviewees to better
discuss their experiences in detail.

In terms of conducting social research on the Internet,
sociologist of science and technology Christine Hine has
argued that we are in an experimental moment.[5] The field
of inquiry and the technical platforms are rapidly expanding. For my interests in *Hello Avatar*, I include sites of
engagement that lay beyond the boundary of an online/
offline binary. Thus, I include cross-platform research that
spans face-to-face, online, and otherwise mediated interactions. My position is that any analysis of informants
and their actions must be contextually situated, whether
that be a virtual world, a terrestrial home, or a mobile
phone exchange.

My argument addresses different platforms of networked media. And, I have worked with Katie Andresen,
the book's designer, to formally present multiple views
of media experience while working to keep the book
thematically and visually focused. Each chapter of *Hello
Avatar* is followed by an interview with a person whose
practice with networked media informs the discussion of
X-reality engagement; interviews with author Cory Doctorow and virtual reality inventor Jaron Lanier are among
the ones presented. The interviews serve as a coda to my
argument in which practitioners and designers speak
directly about their media engagement and the cultures
around it. My purpose with these interviews is to give the
reader a first-person view of the issues discussed. The book
also contains a section of avatar and virtual world figures,
a graphic timeline, and glossary.

Tutoyer: *The You of the Networked Generation*
Throughout this project I have been careful to address
what is "here and now" in terms of technical capability.
I focus my attention on media practice primarily in the
North American and Western European nexus. Not every
example depends on broadband Internet connectivity

or access to expensive technology such as smartphones. This book addresses accelerated media use and design, with an eye toward innovative practices coming from other worlds as well—the virtual and the emerging— from which we might learn.

I spend most of my analysis discussing what has happened during two intense periods of virtual design, 1995–2002 and 2003–2011, in order to create a larger picture of the intersecting technical and cultural fields that have brought us to this moment. In terms of the global culture of networked subjects, regional and national groups demonstrate different behaviors and mores in regard to virtuality and its representations. The values of avatar realism, mobile access to online worlds, as well as the general societal level of comfort around such configurations vary greatly from country to country. For example, North American and Central European countries share media preferences more similar to one another than they do with South Korea or the People's Republic of China. That said, there is also cross-talk between user groups that spans national borders because the ideas and players circulate so quickly.

In addition to the geographic and cultural boundaries of the project, throughout the book I use different forms of address to underscore the various modes of engagement I describe. For example, I use the direct address of *you*, the informal second-person language of traditional interactive adventure text games. This you is a procedural one; it is the you in "You are moving through a murky dungeon and see a door. What do you do?" As well, I move between *I* and *we* in the text to distinguish between my argument as the author and the we of the larger culture in which we all participate. I claim the plural subject of we in relation to a networked subject on the grounds that in an age of media in transition, we are all affected by the change even if, individually, we do not use a particular medium.

Chapter Overview
Chapter 1, "What Is an Avatar?", presents a history of avatars.

6. Marshall McLuhan, *Understanding Media* (Cambridge, MA: MIT Press, 1994), 264. "The invention of the telephone was an incident in the larger effort of the past century to render speech visible," writes McLuhan on the efforts of Melville Bell, father of the telephone inventor Alexander Graham Bell, to create a language called Visible Speech and the influence that work had on his son. Also see Avital Ronell's work on the telephone as a haunted technology, *The Telephone Book: Technology, Schizophrenia, Electric Speech* (Lincoln: University of Nebraska Press, 1991).

My focus is the place of the actual in lives that are increasingly framed by media that is real-time, visual, and simulates presence. I address the history of embodied agents in human-computer interaction (HCI) and raise issues of mediated presence. In a world of accelerated mediation, I ask how we might understand the face-to-face encounter.

Chapter 2, "Putting a Face on Things", outlines the evolution of computer simulated virtual worlds from the text-based to the graphic. I discuss the changes in visualization technologies that accompany an increasingly pervasive media use. I address the new behaviors characterized by the rise of the X-reality media by thinking about the consequences of virtual embodiment in terms of cognitive perception of simulation and cultural reception. Chapter 3, "Interview with the Virtual Cannibal," dives into the virtual world of one player. I explore issues of identity, ethics, virtual violence, and actual consequences in an accelerated media culture.

Chapter 4, "Presence," focuses on research in mediated presences (copresence) and looks at experimental work in virtual reality (VR) labs. I address issues such as behavioral modeling and identity manipulation created with avatar interfaces. In Chapter 5, "X-Reality: A Conclusion," I close with recent work in media forms that contribute innovative design in extending the networked subject's reach across worlds.

Networked Subject

New media technologies have always offered the fantastic while conforming to the needs of daily life when adopted. When it was first introduced, the telephone purported to offer everything from séances with the dead to the piping-in of live entertainment. Over time its uses proved not so fantastic and the telephone grew more and more domesticated in its use.[6]

With virtual worlds, live video chat, and mobile technologies, today we are witnessing the first major shift in synchronous distance communication platforms since the invention of the telephone over one hundred years ago. We possess increasing capability to collaborate with people in what feels like a face-to-face manner, across great distances and in real time.[7] This, then, is the cultural moment this book is about: how we make connections with networked media and the practices we have created around those connections. The lead actor in this drama of expanded horizons is the networked subject—all of us who represent aspects of ourselves and of our work across an ever-expanding mediascape.

7. I would address fax (or facsimile) technology, which is the optical scanning of a document for transmission, as an additional use of the telephone or radio as opposed to a new medium. In 1865, the first telefax services were initiated, preceding the invention of the telephone, but in contemporary times, by the 1970s, telephone wires became the primary mode of sending a fax. Electronic faxes allow for immediate information exchange, but lack the dynamism of form that describes real-time media. They are a fixed medium, a facsimile, being transmitted at an accelerated pace.

What Is an Avatar?

Networked Gathering
On a warm Wednesday evening in Austin, Texas, midway through January 2006, Philip Rosedale, then CEO of Linden Lab, the inventors of Second Life (SL) virtual world, and a group of marketing executives sat together at a dinner party. The dinner followed a day-long seminar on the role of games in the burgeoning market of interactive media. In the laid-back atmosphere of the Tex-Mex margarita joint, the group stuck out not on account of its members' corporate attire among the cowboy hats, but rather for an activity colloquially known as "geeking out." Interspersed with the normal dinner conversation, they huddled together in small groups to watch, comment on, and occasionally type commands into the laptop computers they had on hand. Open on their screens was the digital vista of Second Life, a world made only of information, networked across a series of computer servers.

During the winter of 2006, there were 200,000 Second Life users. By 2008 over seven million people had visited the virtual world. Stories on the virtual world had appeared on the cover of *Newsweek*, in lifestyle and financial pages

1. Real-time means syn-
chronous perception
of an activity or thing
as opposed to asyn-
chronous perception.
For example, a phone
call is real-time but a
film is asynchronous.
Networked media has
begun to conflate the
two categories, but one
can still make basic
distinctions between
the two states in terms
of the technical affor-
dances of a platform.

2. Physicist Albert-
László Barabási de-
veloped the important
concept of scale-free
networks that explains
why points of connec-
tivity organize in hubs
as opposed to even
distribution. Albert-
László Barabási, *Linked:
How Everything Is
Connected to Everything
Else and What it Means
for Business, Science,
and Everyday Life* (New
York: Plume, 2003);
Albert-László Barabási,
Mark Newman, and
Duncan J. Watts,
*The Structure and
Dynamics of Networks*
(Princeton, New Jersey:
Princeton University
Press, 2006).

3. Sociologist Manuel
Castells discusses a
net-work society that
re-distributes the power
of economies, identity,
and nationality on ac-
count of the horizontal
skew of self-organizing
societal networks. Man-
uel Castells, *The Rise
of the Network Society:
The Information Age:
Economy, Society and
Culture*, vol. 1 (Malden,
MA: Wiley-Blackwell
2000).

of the *Wall Street Journal* and *New York Times*, and it
had been the subject of a dinner party at the Davos World
Economic forum. On Google Trends, a search volume index,
Second Life peaked at six million queries in 2007 and came
to near zero—a flatline by early 2011. The hype cycle had
run itself out. Second Life promised something a good
number of people had been interested in investigating: a
second life where they could look like and act like whatever
they chose by using a digital avatar.

In contemporary language an avatar is a computer-
generated figure controlled by a person via a computer. It is
often a graphical representation of a person with which one
can interact in real-time.[1] I make the case for an expanded
definition of avatar that includes a wider array of media
forms and platforms such as Voice over Internet Protocol
(VoIP), instant messaging (IM) and short message service or
text messaging (SMS), and uses of social and locative media.
I argue a broader scope of avatar activity in order to understand better how we are engaging current networked media.

I use the term "networked media" to describe technologies that are connected to a distributed transmission
network such as the Internet or cell towers. In such a case,
"networked" speaks to a technical affordance. However, I
also use the term to invoke a cultural sense of connectivity
with one another. Network theory outlines a set of behaviors
to which a variety of systems—technical, natural, or social—
adhere. One of the primary characteristics of a network is its
distributed rather than hierarchical structure. As opposed to
a regimented order, network connections can happen across
nodal points in a multitude of directions.[2, 3] A networked
gathering then, as I attribute it, involves both a technical
and cultural sense of "networked." In the cultural dimension
of network, the great shift I see is the connection between
online and offline experiences.

Over the span of its visibility and eventual niche rein-
statement, what Second Life actually delivers is not so
much an escape to another life but rather an experience
networked across virtual and real engagement. Like other
emerging media technologies of the early twenty-first

century that possess the qualities of real-time interactions, visualization and a sense of inhabiting space together, the virtual world offered everyday media users an experience that was neither entirely virtual nor real but *vividly actual*. Despite appearances, the members of the dinner party were not so much exhibiting antisocial behavior as intensified hypersocial behavior. At the same moment they gathered in Austin Texas, Lawrence Lessig, an Internet scholar and intellectual property lawyer based in Stanford, California at the time, stood in Second Life, reading from his book, *Free Culture*—actually, a three-dimensional simulation of Lessig—his avatar—stood at a virtual podium and addressed an audience of Second Life denizens, some of whom were sitting hundreds of miles away in Austin (see figures 1.1 to 1.4).

One of the members of the Austin party was a round-faced Jewish planning executive. In Second Life he appeared as a trim African freedom fighter dressed in a tuxedo, sitting in the front row of the virtual amphitheater, enjoying the talk and, from time to time, doing in-game chatting with friends. But perhaps it was Rosedale's seamless overlapping of dinner-party banter and his role as master of virtual ceremonies that best demonstrated this peculiarly contemporary paradox—he was actually in two places at once. Here was a magic trick I wanted to understand.

A virtual world exists on a computer server, or, a series of servers configured to allow many people to simultaneously access the same information. The network effect of a virtual world allows real-time interactions among the players. This means we can have synchronous conversations and direct feedback. Built of computer code, a virtual world presents to players persistent information about where they are, what is happening, and what things look like. Text-based virtual worlds are now more than twenty years old. For text-based worlds, visualization takes place in the imagination as one must read through descriptions of fellow players and the context. In graphical worlds, the computer network generates an image that everyone can see. Additionally, when I add something to the world, e.g., a new room

Reading *Free Culture*: Avatar Mien
Shirakawa sits on Democracy Island in
Second Life, reading a virtual copy of
Free Culture by Lawrence Lessig. Credit:
Johan S, Creative Commons License

Fig.1.1

Portal between worlds: Lawrence Lessig
is reading *Free Culture* in Second Life,
with his avatar standing at the front of
the amphitheater while his live image
is broadcast via video stream. Credit:
Rich115, Creative Commons License

Fig.1.2

A Participant's view: Lawrence Lessig's
book reading in Second Life, as seen
by an audience member. Credit: thelas-
tminute, Creative Commons License

Fig.1.3

Virtual star power: Avatars of author
Lawrence Lessig, founding Second Life
CEO Philip Rosedale, and embedded vir-
tual world journalist Wagner James Au
at Lessig's Second Life reading. Credit:
Rich115, Creative Commons License

Fig.1.4

4. For a discussion of the emerging field platform studies, see the introduction to Nick Montfort and Ian Bogost, *Racing the Beam: The Atari Video Computer System* (Cambridge, MA: MIT Press, 2009).

to a dungeon or a red hat on my avatar's head, everyone can see that virtual space or object as well.

That night in Austin, I witnessed a networked gathering. Walking up and down the aisles of the amphitheater, I saw a siren decked out in a skin-tight pantsuit and platforms, a creature that had a fox-like furry face and human body, and an array of characters who looked as though they had walked right out of a cyberpunk novel with their wild clothes, mohawks and vaguely futurist accoutrement. As far as I could tell, everyone had beautifully fit and perfectly sculpted avatar bodies, even the creature with the fur mug. Dressed that day in business casual, in the virtual world CEO Philip Rosedale sported spiky brown hair, a Rolling Stones red lips T-shirt, and custom jeans with a gem codpiece. In the Second Life world, he appeared cooler than in life. The general feel of the assembled avatars exuded a carefully groomed, hip lifestyle; a combination of experimental hair cuts, flashy clothing and perfectly fit bodies. Above the head of each avatar floated a sign box, announcing avatar names and local affiliations.

How we got to the Lessig reading, that is, the technical infrastructure that enabled this rich graphic environment, was secondary. On the user's end, the only stipulation for being there was a robust Internet connection and a Second Life account which, at the minimum level of participation, is free. On the server side, what we saw before us was five years of development by Linden Lab come to term, the technical issues having faded into the background. Why people chose to be there was the first question that came to my mind. This gathering made clear three traits of networked media that I came to see across the different platforms I investigated: the extension of communication, community, and collaborative systems.

When I use the word "platform" to describe networked media, I am referencing what a technology can do: its attributes and behaviors, along with the implicit cultural protocols built into its design.[4] In this sense, software, a virtual world, and an actual city all represent types of platforms. The cultural protocol of a technology, as defined by media scholar Lisa Gitelman, describes how users adopt and adapt platforms.[5] I argue that the networked tools available for everyday use provide technological affordances of real-time connectivity and visualization that have not been previously available. The adoption of the technologies and their integration into the fabric of daily life reflect new behaviors of engagement that we have created. I am not arguing for a technological determinism where the platform makes the user. Rather, I am suggesting a combinatory practice where platform design influences types of use and users influence the platform design.

In *The Practice of Everyday Life*, sociologist Michel de Certeau introduces the idea of studying quotidian practices as critical to understanding our lives and the society in which we live. In that work, he looks at how people reformulate the objects, places, and languages of their settings to make them habitable.[6] De Certeau uses the analogy of a rented apartment to describe how people take a borrowed space and transform it into a place of their own. In this book I look at daily practices around networked media. I describe and analyze changes in both the design of new media platforms and the cultures we have developed around their engagement. I am calling this change X-reality, which describes the mutual impact of real and mediated engagement.

X-Reality: How Are Your Worlds Colliding?

I am calling this sense of being in two places at once X-reality, by which I mean an interlacing of virtual and real experiences. Traditionally "x" as a prefix has meant "cross," where one finds a bridge between one thing and another. For example, cross-reality design, a category within pervasive computing, describes primarily sensor networks that informationally connect real spaces to virtual ones.[7] I am reappropriating the x of X-reality to stand for an x-factor or variable, as it would in an equation. In positing an X-reality, I am advocating for multidirectional and multivalent understanding of the nature of pervasive media. In this sense, X-reality describes a world that is no longer

5. Lisa Gitelman, *Always Already New: Media, History, and the Data of Culture* (Cambridge, MA: MIT Press 2006).

6. Michel de Certeau, *The Practice of Everyday Life*, trans. Steven Rendall (Berkeley: University of California Press Berkeley, 1984).

7. Beth Coleman, "Using Sensor Inputs to Affect Virtual and Real Environments," *IEEE Pervasive Computing 8*, no. 3, (July–Sept 2009): 16–23.

distinctly virtual or real but, instead, representative of a diversity of network combinations. With X-reality, I mark a turn toward an engagement of networked media integrated into daily life, perceived as part of a continuum of actual events. This is a movement away from computer-generated spaces, places, and worlds that are notably outside of what we might call real life and a transition into a mobile, real-time, and pervasively networked landscape.

As discussed above, I take de Certeau's idea of quotidian practices and ask what happens when daily life now includes a culture of pervasive networked media. Despite the fact that I am a lifelong fan of the comic book heroes the X-Men (a global group of mutants who, on a regular basis, save the world from super villains), my use of X-reality is staunchly, even stodgily placed in the practices of everyday media use. The field studies, research initiatives, and design perspectives I discuss excavate a sense and sensibility of the actual—not real or virtual but the networked media experiences that are now embedded in much of daily life.

Over the last decades of Internet use, terms such as "virtual reality," "cyberspace," and "online" represent a form of engagement that stands outside of the geographically and corporally bounded world we occupy. With the concept of X-reality, I see an end of the virtual or more precisely an end of the binary logic of virtual and real. What has emerged from our collective use of networked technologies is an engagement that moves across sites that are real, simulated, and variously augmented.

Despite the fact of being geographically dispersed, the visual presence of the people assembled at the Second Life event, in the form of avatars, gave the feeling that we were all there at the place. We have had the mediated experience of being in the same time with each other, being temporally synchronous as it were. Many of us have participated in rapid fire email or IM sessions where one person may be in Tokyo and the other New York, but the online conversation happens simultaneously. The thirteen-hour time difference disappears.

Avatars came to the Second Life reading because Lessig's work in the real world resonated for participants in the virtual one.[8] They had not left the material world to forget about the lives they lead. In fact, they had gathered in a virtual space to better converse on worldly issues. Lessig's reading only increased the experience of mediated simultaneity: not only did we reach across geographic timelines, as the Internet does, but we also seemed to arrive at the same place together at the level of sensory perception. This real-time and shared visualized space gave the reading a very similar function to that it would have in the real world. We could listen together and discuss in real time.[9] The emergence of X-reality engagement of networked media presses the question that virtual reality (VR) and virtual environments opened up a decade before: how are your worlds colliding?

X-Reality Media Design
A point that I want to make clear from the outset is that the experience of being two places at once, a mediated presence, is not contingent upon a seamless experience of computing simulation. While aspiring to 3D graphical realism, the Second Life platform of 2006 presented a world in which humanoid avatars were animated with stiff, robotic gestures while the built environment had the affect of a cartoon, more rounded and vague than a building or car would be in a photographic representation.

Comparatively, Second Life was not as graphically beautiful or as easy to use as other networked game platforms of the time (World of Warcraft was moving toward an 11 million unique user number and had a compelling graphical design). Nonetheless, Second Life offered a unique prospect: build the world you want and share it with others. The first generation of Second Life users understood the platform to be an invitation to engage in a shared virtual environment as a maker and not only a player. And it was this combination of the technical affordances of the platform—its collaborative design—and the limits of that design in terms of graphical representation, movement,

8. In his book, Lessig gives a progressive legal theory and cultural analysis on information technologies, creative culture, and intellectual property. He argues for less hindering legislation and better tools with which to make the media culture more free—to establish a public context for creative expression that does not unduly burden citizens with onerous intellectual property laws. Lawrence Lessig, *Free Culture: The Nature and Future of Creativity* (New York: Penguin, 2005).

9. At that time in Second Life, communication existed in a text-only format. We could chat publicly by typing into the main text window and see everyone's conversation scroll down the screen. Or we could send private notes to individuals via an instant messaging (IM) channel. Lessig's avatar "talked" in text to chitchat with the crowd. His video image and audio streamed live into the world for those parts of *Free Culture* that he read.

and the underlying computing of the environment that
informed the nature of the environment. The built aspects
felt entirely artificial and the communicative aspects, how
people engaged each other via avatar, felt largely natural.
How could this networked gathering feel totally artificial and strangely familiar at the same time? The world
before me appeared at once graphically rich and physically
awkward. There was a strange mismatch of personal affects as the avatars wore specialized clothes and adopted
customized gestures, yet moved with inhumanly clipped
gates. The roughness of the motion controls made each of
us seem a bit like the acutely nearsighted cartoon character Mr. Magoo—we were all crashing into walls or each
other, and the like. Yet, despite the hitches and glitches, the
scene held the attention of those of us both at the Austin
dinner party and also in Second Life. I found that this
three-dimensional forum had been leveraged as a communication tool. Even more strikingly, I realized a community
had manifested before my eyes. Many of the people who
gathered hailed one another as they would upon entering
a neighborhood coffee house. These avatars carried the air
of habitués, people who frequented the place. By meeting
in this manner they did not seek novelty (at least not as
an end unto itself), they sought camaraderie. One could
see Second Life in terms of the traditions of text-based
networked worlds that hailed from the 1990s when people
first populated sites called multi-user dungeons (MUDs),
and where community building defined people's engagement as opposed to game playing per se.

The graphical setting itself demonstrated the collaborative and community aspect of the gathering. All of
the virtual objects displayed—amphitheater, avatars, and
event—added up to a giant collaborative effort. Additionally, each person participating had constructed a unique
avatar sitting in the audience. Using a mouse and computer control pad, anyone could move around the space,
navigating depth, height, and speed. All of these traits
together—three-dimensional properties of the scene, the
unique avatars, the real-time expression—created a feeling

of actual place and presence despite the fact that we were far away from a world of photorealism or human movement. Behind each flashy avatar sat a real person at a computer screen, all typing away furiously in the midst of conversation. We were practicing a mode of face-to-face communication where the avatars were the form of mediation.

10. Norbert Wiener, *Cybernetics: or the Control and Communication in the Animal and the Machine* (Cambridge: MIT Press, 1965); *The Human Use of Human Beings* (New York: Da Capo Press, 1988).

C3 of Networked Media: Communication, Community, and Collaboration

The Lessig reading in Second Life demonstrated what I came to see as the C3 of networked media: communication, community, and collaboration. In 1948, Norbert Wiener, the founder of cybernetics, established a C3 configuration for that science that relied on a command-control-communications structure of human-machine relations.[10] As the primary innovation of a cybernetic system versus a mechanical one, Wiener underscored feedback, i.e., in cybernetics, information cycles between the actors in the system and does not just move from the top down or in a unilateral direction. In this concept of feedback as circulation, people and things have impact on each other. As the workplace and the home became more automated, human beings could also perceive themselves as part of a larger system of exchanges.

In his C3 structure for cybernetics, Wiener predicted the emergence of a distributed communication system that forecast the kind of network connection we find with the Internet. In his grand vision of a cybernetics relay system, Wiener included relay models as diverse as the automotive factory floor and the human nervous system. His vision spanned systems from the human-machine interface to the biological. He focused on the ability to relay information in newly founded configurations and speeds, which indicated a turn from hierarchical systems of command to distributed ones in which every participant in the chain of information could be an intelligent one.

In this very particular sense, machines gained a new status beyond the dumb things of the mechanical age and

well before the scientific conversation regarding artificial
intelligence (AI) began. Since the 1950s high point of cybernetics, we had already begun, as a culture, to practice an
animated exchange with machines that was neither human
communication nor entirely mechanical. Down the road,
the emerging automation of machine intelligence would
come to a massive scale of development with the adoption
of computers and computing software. These early cybernetic feedback systems of anti-aircraft artillery (that Wiener
worked on) and radar (an invention of the Second World
War) spoke of a distributed communication system based
on technical models of feedback and statistical prediction
that changed the nature of communication, be it in warfare
or business or pleasure. In cybernetics one finds a graduated
reorganization of information systems and social structure,
each influencing the other. Networked new media practice
amplifies the scale and pace of this reorganization.

The C3 structure of networked media builds on the
idea of intelligent feedback that cybernetics proposed and
the Internet manifests. Beyond what we have seen with
existing network practice, the new generation of networked
media offers to extend the boundaries of participation.
Increasingly, we have the ability to work together at the
same time, no matter where we are, and, in a single visualized space. People have spoken to each other via media
extensions such as the telephone for over a hundred years.
But in this case, networked communication media offers
the potential for directly engaged action—an immediate
collaboration between agents—that has not existed previously outside of the actual experience of working in the
same lab or living in the same locale. Networked media
offers a possibility of engagement that had previously been
limited to the domain of face-to-face interaction. This is an
experience in networked media we have not had before.

Real-time processes, the experience of a synchronous
or live network connection, present an important addition
to our tools of expression. In the past decade, we find an
expanding array of media designed for real-time interaction,
e.g., VoIP, IM, SMS, computer game engines, and locative

media. All of these formats enable synchronous exchanges. In the history of bilateral (two-way) communication, we have had live voice and text connection and on occasion, as with video conferencing, a live two-way channel on video stream. Synchronous network exchanges invoke the sensation of being together across lines of mediation, which is called "copresence." In a shared virtual space, you see my avatar and wave to me, in real time. Likewise, I wave back at your avatar. Regardless of the purpose of the encounter, whatever it is we are doing, we are doing it together.

In our daily lives we do not think twice about such a simple exchange or gesture leading to conversation. However, the capacity to perform such an exchange with ease and grace in a virtual reality has been years in the making. Even as real-time exchanges have augmented our perception of being together virtually, the experience of copresence has become increasingly important to how we sustain communities (see figures 1.5 and 1.6).

From its Latinate root ("com"), community means together. Beyond the etymological origin, it is very difficult to find a consensus today on what defines a community. Traditionally defined as a group of people interacting in a common location, community in many ways determines our basic concept of what it means to participate in a society.[11] With the dawning of distributed networks for communication technologies, we find a profoundly altered landscape from any traditional concept of community. In other words, community can be formed by affiliation, not merely location. Enabled by the current offering of media platforms that support real-time functions and experiences of copresence, we now have a powerful battery of connective applications and connected devices available.

Midway through the last century, and in light of accelerated automation of machine systems, Wiener had phrased the question of technological change and societal transition in the following terms: what is the human use of human beings? With the dawning of pervasive networked media, the question we may now ask ourselves is: how shall

11. For a classic sociological distinction between community and society, see Ferdinand Tönnies, *Community & Society* (Gemeinschaft und Gesellschaft), translated and edited by C. Loomis (East Lansing: Michigan State University Press, 1957). For contemporary discussion of community with focus on Western community formation see D. W. McMillan and D. M. Chavis, "Sense of Community: A Definition and Theory," *Journal of Community Psychology 14* (January 1986); R. Putnam, *Bowling Alone: The Collapse and Revival of American Community* (New York: Simon & Schuster, 2000); M. A. Canuto and J. Yaeger, eds., *The Archaeology of Communities* (New York: Routledge, 2000).

Virtual gathering: iCommons meeting
in Second Life with live video stream.
Credit: rikomatic's photostream, Creative Commons License

Fig.1.5

Birds of a feather: Creative Commons
Second Life event brings together avatars Cornelius Linden, Lawrence Lessig,
and a virtual Cory Doctorow, writer and
an editor of the blog Boing Boing, pup-
peteered by Wagner James Au, March
2006. Credit: Wagner James Au

Fig.1.6

12. A. Gopnik, A. Melt-
zoff, and P. Kuhl, *The
Scientist in the Crib:
What Early Learning
Tells Us about the
Mind* (New York:
Harper, 2000).

we come together? Given the affordances of the media,
what are the X-reality spaces we make? In creating new
practices around media engagement, almost invariably, the
first way in which we begin to answer such questions is by
trying to fathom what it means to come face-to-face by way
of mediation.

By "face-to-face," I mean people interacting in the same
geographic and physically embodied location. By "mediated,"
I am addressing a fairly literal idea of technological mediation such as telephone or Internet. At this time I am not
taking up the more philosophical question as to whether
or not we can encounter each other in an unmediated way
even when we meet face-to-face. That said, in my argument
with regard to X-reality platforms, I see an increasingly pervasive presence of mediation in our everyday lives. Face-to-
face encounters remain central to our lives, but networked
media increasingly augments them.

Affordances of Embodiment
On first blush, faces offer an irresistible attractor. They are
what babies first look at before they can take in the rest of
the world.[12] They are the unique imprints of the people we
love. As it turns out, faces on computers may elicit similar
fascination, even as they can provoke distress.

When a face or figure appears on your screen (often as
the primary mode of engagement with a machine program)
you see before you an embodied agent. Also known as a
"software agent" or an "intelligent agent," an embodied
agent was a low-level, artificial intelligence (AI) program
that used various technical strategies such as databases of
human language, motion and facial expression recognition
to respond to human interlocutors. Instead of a command
line with a cursor or an icon that you click, an embodied
agent might greet you and respond to your queries. People
nicknamed these creatures "chatbots" for their role as
conversational agents, i.e., robotic or automated conversationalists. Embodied agents represent a period of computer
science research in which the newly acquired capabilities
of computer-generated imaging (CGI) intersected with the

exuberance of AI research.

By the end of the 1990s, researchers internationally engaged in a concerted effort to make computers more humanlike, or at least easier to use. Embodied agents were meant to change the human-computer interaction (HCI) as dramatically as adding icons to computer interface did a decade before that.[13] Striving for an interface device beyond the iconic, for many researchers the natural progression in humanizing machines was to give them faces.[14] The thought was that the power of adding a face to a machine could transform communication media. In retrospect, they were wrong. Putting a face on things, software in this case, failed to make interaction with a computer more effective.

In their 2000 article, "More Than Just a Pretty Face: Affordances of Embodiment," HCI researcher Justine Cassell, then at the MIT Media Lab, along with members of her research group Tom Bickmore, Hannes Vilhjálmsson, and Yan Hao assess the value of using humanlike faces and conversation in computer interface design.[15] On this subject Cassell and her collaborators write: "The qualitative differ-ence...is not just that we enjoy looking at humans more than at computer screens but also that the human body... provide[s] for a more rich and robust channel of commu-nication than is afforded by any other medium available today."[16] They underscore the idea that embodied figures communicate better, but with one important caveat. Cassell and her research group argue that virtual embodi-ment provides better communication only if human con-versation accompanies it.[17]

Looking like someone must also have the quality of acting like someone, or the feeling of connection is lost. Embodiment does not only mean having a particular appear-ance; it also means behaving in particular ways. Our expec-tations regarding intelligence, feedback, and responsiveness of a humanlike interlocutor need to be met. The gestures of humanness, the possibility of give-and-take in a con-versation and, in short, the affective qualities of dialogue must accompany an embodied agent for it to be an actual conversational partner. The fact that embodied agents did

13. When Apple, Xerox PARC, and other com-puting technology companies of the 1980s introduced an icon-based interface, the pictorial interac-tion largely replaced the command-line input required by the DOS operating system. This change in HCI design—how we engage with a machine—had tremendous impact on both popularizing personal computers and making us feel at home in using them.

14. Literature in HCI design supporting the complexity of engaging with humanoid icons includes S. Keisler and L. Sproull, "'Social' Human-Computer Interaction," in *Human Values and the Design of Computer Technol-ogy*, ed. B. Friedman (New York: Cambridge University Press, 1997), 191–200; T. Koda and P. Maes, "Agents with Faces: The Effect of Personification of Agents," *Proceedings of the Fifth IEEE In-ternational Workshop on Robot and Human Communication* (RO-MAN '96): 189–194; K. R. Thórisson, "Commu-nicative Humanoids: A Computational Model of Psychosocial Dialogue Skills," PhD thesis, MIT Media Laboratory, 1996; A. Takeuchi and T. Naito, *Situated Facial Dis-plays: Towards Social Interaction*, in *Human Factors in Comput-ing Systems: CHI'95 Conference Proceedings*, ed. I. R. Katz, R. Mack, L. Marks, M. B. Rosson, and J. Nielsen (New York: ACM Press), 450–455.

15. Justine Cassell, Tom Bickmore, Hannes Vilhjálmsson, and Yan Hao, "More Than Just a Pretty Face: Affordances of Embodiment," *Proceedings of the Fifth International Conference on Intelligent User Interfaces* ACM (2000): 52.

16. Ibid., 1.

17. See also W. Lewis Johnson and Jeff W. Rickel, "Animated Pedagogical Agents: Face-to-Face Interaction in Interactive Learning Environments," *International Journal of Artificial Intelligence in Education* (2000) no. 11: 47–78; Justine Cassell, Joseph Sullivan, Scott Prevost, Elizabeth F. Churchill, ed., *Embodied Conversational Agents* (Cambridge, MA: MIT Press, 2000).

18. Cassell et al., "More Than Just a Pretty Face," 1.

19. Ben Schneiderman, *Leonardo's Laptop: Human Needs and the New Computing Technologies* (Cambridge: MIT Press, 2002).

not become popular forms has everything to do with the analysis that the Cassell group tenders: human likeness in voice or appearance also calls for human responsiveness, which is a very difficult feat for a computer program to pull off.

Cassell's insights remain important today for what it can tell us about how we engage avatars—the graphical humanesque figures that move across our various screens. The key difference is that we are now putting a face on things—creating embodied figures for avatars—to facilitate human-to-human conversation via mediation. In "More Than Just a Pretty Face," Cassell and her colleagues critique the culture of embodied agents and urge designers to take into account aspects of behavioral interaction beyond the visual signal.

The crucial insight we gain from Cassell and her group is their attempt to incorporate human-communication protocols into HCI design. The design goal is not to replace face-to-face conversation with computer-mediated communication, but to make the *simulation* of face-to-face far more satisfying. We have arrived at a moment when mediation is embedded in daily life. The point of greatest transformation is not human and computer relations, but human-to-human engagement.

Face-to-Face

In the HCI scientific literature as well as in the common sense of daily practice, one finds the general assumption that face-to-face communication is always superior to technologically mediated communication. In "More Than Just a Pretty Face: Affordances of Embodiment," Cassell states this proposition directly, "If you have something important to say you say it face-to-face."[18] Ben Shneiderman, who has helped to lead the field in HCI and information visualization, concurs.[19] The thought is that technological mediation fails to replicate the nuance, touch, and multisensory experience of a face-to-face encounter. Computer science during the 1990s aspired to simulate a seamless communication between embodied agent (software agent and intelligent agent) and user, but the technology could not effectively engage a human interlocutor. In more recent work, similar terms of verisimilitude in visualization, real-time exchange, and signaling have been brought to bear in framing the work on telepresence design.[20]

If we shift the frame on the conception of mediated face-to-face engagement away from intelligent software to a sociological view of people addressing each other across media channels, we find a very different perspective on the valuation of face-to-face interaction, and particularly in regard to mobile telephony. To begin with, perfect simulation is not a baseline requirement for meaningful communication.

Working with the technologies in hand (spotty cell phone connectivity, low bandwidth for sending images or live VoIP, minimal opportunity for email or a network connection), in each case we find that people seize upon the opportunities to extend sites of connectivity and bring, with all manner of resourcefulness, a great capacity to weed through the noisiness of a media signal to find the message being sent. Sociologists of communication media Stefana Broadbent and Richard Ling have demonstrated in their research that as a society we use forms of mediated communication pervasively and most often with those with whom we are most intimate.[21]

Participatory Culture

Over the past few decades, much of the analysis of digital media finds that it lowers the threshold for communication, material reproduction, creative expression, and civic engagement. In comparison to industrial economies and mass media infrastructure, one finds digital media platforms characterized by modularity, recombination, and easy distribution.[22] Personal computing, an individual's access to a networked computer console, defines the material practice that supported this societal shift. Social network sites, blogs, online video, and shared music sites all represent modes of popular expression that are coinages of this moment in digital reproduction and networked media exchange.

20. Sandy Pentland's work on expressive human signals, which he calls "honest" signals, relates primarily to face-to-face encounters and how they can be interpreted via a technological interface (a sensor-enabled wearable computing device). In conditions of network mediation, Judith Donath's research on signaling and Jeffrey T. Hancock's work on lying on social networks address the primarily the inability of media to convey an accurate image or message of its user.

21. Stefana Broadbent, "Transforming the home," Usage Watch: Observing the evolution of technology usage, December 2010, <http://usagewatch.org/detail. php?idcat=3&id=187>; "How the Internet Enables Intimacy," TEDGlobal, July 2009, <http://www.ted.com/talks/stefana_broadbent_how_the_internet_enables_intimacy.html>. Richard Ling and Jonathan Donner, *Mobile Communication* (Malden, MA: Polity 2009).

22. Lev Manovich's *Language of New Media* (Cambridge, MA: MIT Press, 2002) offers a primer on the technical and cultural attributes of digital new media.

23. Nicholas Carr, *The
Shallows: What the
Internet Is Doing to
Our Brains* (New York:
W. W. Norton & Com-
pany, 2010).

Cooperation has become one of the most powerful signs
of the changes wrought by networked media. In *The Wealth
of Networks* (2004), media theorist and legal scholar Yochai
Benkler discusses the paradigm shift from an industrial
economy to an information economy in terms of the potential of cooperative network practices, such as the open
source software movement. Benkler points to the acceleration of peer production networks for which individuals
form loose communities around a topic of interest, as the
primary source of innovation for contemporary society. He
attributes the shift from an industrial economy to a network
economy primarily to the development of cooperative networks within which people share information.

Following the early years of enthusiasm around the
cooperative potential of networked media, as Benkler
describes, we find ourselves in a state of backlash. Critics
of cooperative network practices, such as Nicholas Carr,
have launched attacks on the value of content and cognitive
aspects of network engagement finding that, culturally, we
are stuck in an intellectual shallows; the breadth of Internet
connectivity does not facilitate a depth of understanding.[23]
The split Carr describes is between a historical class of
professionals, or the masters of a medium, and an ascending culture of amateurs. In my analysis of network engagement, I am suggesting that this split between a rarefication
of mastery versus a cultural dissolution authored by the
"unwashed" masses presents a false binary.

In framing pervasive media engagement, I believe it
is critical to look at knowledge production and network
engagement in terms of both the technical facility for
broadcast and the cultural authority to participate. In
arguing for a continuum of knowledge productions and
network engagement, I cite the work of media scholar
Henry Jenkins. In describing the Internet as a popular
culture communication network, Jenkins proposes an
understanding of networked media participation that
works outside of the traditional boundaries of professional
versus amateur production.[24] Focusing on the practices of
everyday media users in dialogue with traditional mass

media or industry producers, he understands fans as participants in the production of culture. He calls this interaction between amateur and auteur—new media maker and old media master—a convergence culture. In framing a networked subject, my primary interest in Jenkin's argument on convergence is the role of participation. In my estimation, participation is closely linked to practices of agency and issues of media engagement. Jenkins distinguishes between interactivity as an affordance of technology, while participation describes what people do. As with Benkler, the importance of this distinction rests in an understanding of participation as a driving force in the societal change. If networked media provides the technical platforms for cooperation, it is participation that defines the culture. In a report on digital media and learning for the MacArthur Foundation, Jenkins and his coauthors describe a culture shift in which people engage new media technologies to "archive, annotate, appropriate, and recirculate media content in powerful new ways."[25] Jenkins writes of the powerful ways people change their own lives with quotidian media practices. In discussing networked subjects, I frame self-recognition of ability as a site of agency. To broaden Jenkins' definition, I am suggesting that agency needs to include positions such as listening and being present and not exclusively actions, as such.

I agree with Jenkins that participation frames the contemporary in the same way that we might say the industrial defined the last epoch. But I would qualify the terms of participation to recognize engagement—what I have described as ambient experiences of being present to one another using networked media. Although I discuss activist use of media in other contexts, I am arguing here for a media engagement that is not necessarily based on great activity.[26] We do not have to be fans, code writers, or other forms of devoted participants to engage. We need, in fact, to be present to each other. The terms of networked media engagement are both more subtle and more profound than participation suggests. It is the pervasive aspect of networked media that calls for greater inquiry.

24. Henry Jenkins, *Convergence Culture: Where Old and New Media Collide* (New York: NYU Press, 2007).

25. Henry Jenkins, Katie Clinton, Ravi Purushotma, Alice J. Robison, and Margaret Weigel, *Confronting the Challenges of Participatory Culture: Media Education for the 21st Century*, (Cambridge, MA: MIT Press, 2009).

26. Beth Coleman, "Designing Agency," Designing Learning Futures, Digital Media and Learning conference, Long Beach, CA, March 5, 2011, http://dmlcentral.net/conference2011; Beth Coleman, Michael Ananny, Gilad Lotan, "Tweeting the Revolution," Proceedings: A Decade in Internet Time: Symposium on the Dynamics of the Internet and Society, Oxford Internet Institute, September 2011.

27. Mark Weiser, "The
Computer for the 21st
Century," *Scientific
American* 265, no. 3
(1991):94–104.

28. See Bruce Sterling,
Shaping Things (Cam-
bridge: MIT Press,
2005); Julian Bleeker,
"A Manifesto for Net-
worked Objects: Co-
habiting with Pigeons,
Arphids and Aibos in
the Internet of Things
(Why Things Matter),"
2006, <http://www.
nearfuturelaboratory.
com/2006/02/26/
a-manifesto-for-net-
worked-objects/>.

Ubiquitous Computing

As I have discussed above in my analysis of participatory
media culture, media theorists have characterized the transition from industrial networks of production to the digital
computational model in terms of the wealth of networks
and a language of new media. The substantial difference
one finds thirty years later is the pervasive aspect of
networked media. Its increasing mobility is coupled with
an increasingly consequential relation to space, place, and
time where the physical world and the virtual platform
intersect—what I have described as an X-reality engagement.
In addition to text-based information, aspects of the physical
world are increasingly tethered to a network. The Internet
of Things represents the vision of ubiquitous computing
coming online in popular form. Formulated by HCI chief
scientist Mark Weiser at Xerox PARC in 1988, ubiquitous
computing (ubicomp) has been called the "third wave" of
the computing revolution, where computing culture moves
off the desktop and out into the world.[27]

In a ubicomp world, everything is animated. For
example, we now live in a world where objects count
themselves. Whether it is with radio-frequency identification (RFID) tags or another kind of sensor, one finds
information systems that, in real-time, track objects whose
presence can be read by satellite, radio, or scanner.[28] The
Internet of Things is the name of a growing movement in
ubicomp design in which sensor-linked objects, actions,
and capacities are tethered to a network. In the most basic
terms, the Internet of Things describes a consortium of
designers who are creating sense-able objects that can be
located and interacted with across a network.

Implicit in the logic of the Internet of Things is also an
idea of the sensible object: a formerly "dumb thing" newly
animated with a network intelligence. Then sense of
risk that media scholars and users have expressed relates
directly to the animation of objects in the world. The risk
lies in the prospect that as the thing becomes sensible, the
human subject, as a subject of a network culture, becomes

more thing-like.[29]

What is at stake is the framing of the face-to-face experience, the discernment of the authentic or the real, and the engagement of the subject as agent within a distributed network. I am arguing that we engage pervasive media systems as a regular supplement to face-to-face encounters. The mediation does not substitute for the physical and proximal contact. However, it does provide specific forms of augmentation that are meaningful sites of the actual. My analysis of what is formally and culturally different about networked media from mass media—and even including the first decades of Internet use—hinges on a concept of the actual. In my estimation, the actual describes sites of engagement that are neither real nor virtual but spanning territories. In order to present my conceptualization of the actual, I want first to frame my construction of pervasive media.

29. For an extended analysis of subject and object network animation see, Beth Coleman, "Everything is Animated: Pervasive Media and the Networked Subject" special issue on Animation and Automation, *Body & Society* (in press).

Pervasive Media

In introducing the term pervasive media, I borrow from the language of computer science where pervasive computing, also known as ubicomp, is an established field that looks at computing for an animated world in which objects, places, and gestures are included on a computational network. As discussed above, this is the world of the Internet of Things: a sensor-relay world that has moved beyond the desk-based personal computer and assumes an informational mantle across the environment. With ubicomp the computational work of information processing is integrated into objects, activities, and sites of the everyday. And, again like the HCI aspiration to perfectly simulate a face-to-face encounter, ubicomp has not yet achieved the scale of pervasive computing to which it aims.

In contrast to ubicomp, I use the term pervasive media to describe a global culture that engages a spectrum of networked technologies. I am speaking of technical affordances of platforms such as virtual worlds, voice-over-Internet protocol, mobile rich-media and texting, and microblogging formats such as Twitter. Web-based video (YouTube), social

30. McKenzie Wark, *Virtual Geography: Living with Global Media Events*, (Bloomington: Indiana University Press, 1994), vii.

profile pages (Facebook), and web logs (blogs) figure into my analysis, but often as part of the ecosystem of network use as opposed to being the sites of emergent behavior. I ascribe to this spectrum of media technologies an implicit sense of convergence in which one engages multiple forms for a transmediated communication.

In terms of the technical affordances, my assessment is that networked media, as a whole, simulates presence. If a medium has a message, as McLuhan famously pronounced, then the message of the increasingly real-time, visual, and locative media we engage is: "I am here." Being here does not rely exclusively on a physical instantiation. In other words, neither geographic territory nor corporeal embodiment stand as the exclusive indication of being somewhere, or being present. I am not arguing for an equivalence of lived, bodily experience with our experience of being filtered through an avatar (our networked proxies). I am arguing for recognition of porous spheres of engagement that meet across a continuum of the actual.

In his 1994 book *Virtual Geography*, media theorist McKenzie Wark describes the virtual geography we inherit with the advent of global media. He writes, "We live every day also in another terrain, equally familiar: the terrain created by the television, the telephone, the telecommunications networks crisscrossing the globe. [Virtual geography] is about the expanded terrain from which experience may be instantly drawn."[30] In his argument global media has affected our experience of the world (i.e., where we live locally) and has provided windows into other worlds. Wark describes this as an effect of telesthesia—perception at a distance.

In building from Wark's assessment of the expanded view of virtual geography, I see that it is the status of the subject itself that has shifted with new affordances of technology and emergent cultures around its engagement. What has changed with our virtual geographies has to do with the increased ability to interact remotely. We are not exclusively looking at events from afar with a telescopic gaze but, increasingly, we have the ability to engage. We now have more platforms from which to reach each other, not merely look at something. I am suggesting a shift from virtual geographies to sites of the actual. In this configuration, it is the changing position of agency that is most important to understand in the engagement of networked media. As stated, my definition of pervasive media is not focused on computing systems as much as it is on how people make use of the emergent networked channels to support a self-conception of agency. I want to make clear, however, that the value of the term is not predicated on each individual in every location possessing access to high bandwidth Internet or, for that matter, any connectivity at all.

Anthropologist Genevieve Bell in her work with computer scientist Paul Dourish offers a critique of ubicomp that contributes to the case I am making for understanding pervasive media as quotidian practice and not exclusively as a discourse of technological perfectionism. Bell and Dourish write: "Arguably, though, ubiquitous computing is already here; it simply has not taken the form that we originally envisaged and continue to conjure in our visions of tomorrow."[31] In their analysis they look at the actual "mess" of technology within the "infrastructures of daily life," discussing the ways in which people actually engage networked media as opposed to an HCI vision of idealized simulation and connectivity.[32] In my view, their argument supports a global view of networked media adoption that stands outside of the traditional, neocolonial language of globalization.

If one frames pervasive media exclusively in terms of media networks access, then one simply reiterates an inherited neocolonialist perspective: the neocolonialist view would only recognize those who are fully technologically engaged in media networks to be recognizable in the publics of that culture. There is a growing scholarly community addressing what I am calling pervasive media engagement in respect to global and rural groups. Along with other media globalists, Ethan Zuckerman, Senior Researcher at Berkman Center for Internet and Society and cofounder of the Global Voices blog, has pointed out the potentially treacherous implications of talking of pervasive media.[33]

31. Genevieve Bell and Paul Dourish, "Yesterday's tomorrows: notes on ubiquitous computing's dominant vision," *Personal and Ubiquitous Computing* 11, no. 2 (Spring 2007): 134.

32. Paul Dourish and Genevieve Bell, Divining a Digital Future: Mess and Mythology in Ubiquitous Computing, (Cambridge, MA: MIT Press, 2011).

33. Interview with
Ethan Zuckerman
October 19, 2010, MIT
Media Lab, Cambridge,
MA. Also see, Ethan
Zuckerman, "Genevieve
Bell complicates the
mobile phone," 09/06/
2007 (10:56 pm); "Ke-
nya Matters" 11/19/
2010 (8:38 pm), My
Heart's in Accra,
<http://www.ethan
zuckerman.com/blog/>.

34. Mary L. Gray, Out
in the Country: Youth,
Media, and Queer
Visibility in Rural
America (New York:
NYU Press, 2009).

35. In his work over
the past three decades,
sociologist Manual
Castells has described
a societal shift at the
scale of the global that
marks a transformation
from industrial to net-
work society. Castells
makes the case that
identity, behaviors,
and community are
all affected by the
global adoption of con-
nected communication
technologies in such
a way that historical
power relations, the
authority of the state,
and structures by
which societies have
organized themselves
are in flux. I discuss
this concept at greater
length in chapter 3.

36. Wendy Hui Kyong
Chun, Control and
Freedom: Power and
Paranoia in the Age of
Fiber Optics (Cambridge,
MA: MIT Press, 2006).

37. Sherry Turkle, Alone
Together: Why We Ex-
pect More from Technol-
ogy and Less from Each
Other (New York: Basic
Books, 2011).

Similarly, communication scholar Mary Gray's work on
rural sectors of the United States and media engagement
also helps to open the conversation beyond the idioms of
full connectivity in the rich Western cities. She argues that
queer youth have media presence along with a strong
exchange between online and real-world presence that con-
founds general stereotypes about the critical importance
of an urban setting to express lesbian, gay, bisexual, and
transgendered identities.[34] In my formulation, I am looking
at a pervasive media in the purview of a networked society,
where all are affected by the changes in communication
and mediation even if one does not participate per se.[35]

The importance in broadening the context in which
we understand pervasive media engagement rests in how
we conceptualize agency in the current age. In a network
society, I understand agents are the people formerly known
as users. The implication is one of dependency, addiction,
and, ultimately, objectification where one is conscripted
into the logic of whatever is being used, be it a technology,
drug, etc. User is the opposite of agency, as media theorist
Wendy Chun has pointed out.[36] In my analysis, agency
addresses the possibility of self-determinant action. With
the concept of the networked subject, I posit a theory
of agency that recognizes that we now work across, i.e.,
across platforms and geographies of the virtual and the
real. I see a critical link between the actual and agency
that informs how we engage networked media.

When Media Use Changes the User to Agent

Sociologist of technology Sherry Turkle describes the age of
mobile media as a fugue state of being "alone together." She
casts increased mediation as a causal factor in increased
isolation at a societal scale.[37] I would argue, to the contrary,
that we must view the accelerated mediation of the early
twenty-first century as a repositioning of the subject. I do
not make a technologically determinant argument. It is not
media technologies that reposition us, but rather how we
engage them in a symbiotic relationship. In her critique of
pervasive media engagement, Turkle expresses nostalgia

for a time when media did not so thoroughly immerse us. I would suggest that there is no return to an unmediated world, a bucolic face-to-face exchange, if it ever existed in the first place. In other words, the mandate is to conceptualize the best conditions for the world moving forward since we live with the histories of technology and mediation already in effect.

What we find at this moment in media scholarship, design, and engagement is a split with regard to how the networked subject situates itself. Are we tethered to a system in which we are interpolated as a thing or rendered childlike, as Turkle and virtual reality inventor Jaron Lanier have recently argued (I discuss Lanier's critique and his historic contribution to VR research in chapter 4).[38] Or are we augmented by our media engagement, ascending to new heights of reach and ability as Benkler and Jenkins discuss. I am suggesting a third point of analysis that focuses on practices of networked agency.

We have seen scholarship in online identity, collaboration and crowd sourcing, information exchange, and markets, as the results of networked economies and ecologies. Yet we have seen little or no theorization of what the subject itself is. If everything moves toward being animated in a network society, then we must think anew about the mechanics of agency that we might see beyond a subject simply interpolated into a system of things. Against this impulse, I want to look at possibilities of agency.

Agency

A theory of agency and its mechanics is critical to this investigation. I define agency in terms of how we understand ourselves as actors in an environment, as well as how our effect on such an environment might be gauged. My definition builds on the model of emergent interactive agency defined by psychologist Albert Bandura.[39] He describes a subject that is neither a mechanical instrument, responding slavishly to the environment, nor a fully autonomous monad, perfectly self-determining.[40] Rather, his theory of interactive agency assesses an actor in context. "Personal

38. Jaron Lanier, You Are Not a Gadget (New York: Vintage, 2010).

39. Albert Bandura, *Social Foundations of Thought and Action: A Social Cognitive Theory* (Englewood Cliffs, NJ: Prentice-Hall, 1986).

---

40. Albert Bandura, "Human Agency in Social Cognitive Theory," *American Psychologist* 44, No. 9, (September 1989): 1175–1184.

41. Ibid., 1175.

42. Ibid.

43. James Paul Gee, *What Video Games Have to Teach Us About Learning and Literacy*, Second Edition (New York: Palgrave Macmillan, 2007).

agency," he writes, "operates within the interactional causal structure."[41] He describes a subject contingent on the contextual, yet also self-organizing and capable of self-determining action.

In Bandura's model of agency, the central enabling factor is "people's belief about their capabilities to exercise control over events that affect their lives."[42] He sketches a mechanism of agency that is based on an innerknowledge; a predictive sense that one can affect the world outside oneself. However this innerknowledge is based on a feedback loop between agent and environment. In seeing the results of one's intentions objectified in the world, one confirms a "self-appraisal of capabilities," as Bandura phrases it. I apply Bandura's model of agency to practices of pervasive media with the explicit interest of understanding how we may gauge a subject's effect on an environment as well as a self-appraisal of capabilities.

I offer a model from game design, with an eye toward the complexity of real-world contexts. Computer games, I would suggest, model the interactional logic of self-appraisal in a literal manner. In order to be properly motivated to play through a difficult game, the player needs to know she can meaningfully affect the game environment.[43] Through interacting with the game, the player sees that her efforts have value. The world of the game reflects the player's self-appraisal of agency in such a situation. With the gamer model of agency, we have a finite and knowable context for engagement in comparison with our activities in the world. To discuss the kind of feedback loops of self-appraisal we find in life, we need to better understand how we are situated in our networked media practices.

In my analysis of pervasive media—its use and design, culture and science—I see a subject that is not enthralled by technology. We are not players framed by someone else's game design. Nor are we abject beings overcome by an enveloping apparatus of simulation, which is the devastating scenario films like *A Scanner Darkly* (Linklater, 2006) and *The Matrix* (Larry and Andy Wachowski, 1999) depict. Our engagement with accelerated mediation is less dramatic than either case, and far more divergent in global outlook.[44]

With the figure of the networked subject, I underscore the importance of looking at our media engagement as a form of augmentation where we include rather than demarcate exchanges that exist outside of the normative formulation of the geographically and bodily proximate. In doing so, we gain a clearer perspective on what we do and who we are.

I use the word augmentation to indicate an addition and not, in particular, a positive or negative valuation of that addition.[45] Writer Kevin Kelly discusses the augmented self as a symbiotic relationship with technology.[46] In his assessment, technology has domesticated us. Kelly does not indicate that we are enslaved, but, rather, that we are "coevolving." The idea of coevolving, or, what marks an interrelation between technology and self, supports my conception of technology as augmentation.

If I take an example from popular culture, Steve Austin, protagonist of the 1970s television show *Six Million Dollar Man*, is cybernetically augmented to do fantastic things such as run inhumanly fast, see with telescopic vision and possess superhuman strength. On the other hand, those of us who wear eyeglasses do not necessarily think of ourselves as augmented. Spectacles are sufficiently culturally assimilated that we do not see them as a technology per se. With my examples of the fictive cyborg and the case of vision correction, I point to an extended history of augmenting self and environment. I am suggesting that this moment of boundary crossing, when a technology goes from being explicit and alien to the embedded and acculturated, has arrived for pervasive media technologies. Our task is to critically engage its integration in the world.

Anthropologist of science and technology Lucy Suchman describes the capacity of agency in terms of situated action.[47] In Suchman's formulation the context of an action determines the nature of that action and its effect. She focuses her analysis within the framework of human-machine mediation, addressing the period in computer science when embodied agents were the ascendant goal in the field

44. In saying the network subject is neither enthralled nor abject, I also recognize that coercion, misunderstanding, and malice abound across our mediated networks. I discuss some of the forms of media coercion in chapter 4.

45. I ascribe here to a theory of the supplement, as discussed by philosophers such as Jacques Derrida in regard to language and Bernard Steigler concerning technology, among others, wherein a system of being or a system of knowing includes aspects that are framed in the language of originary (organic) and aspects that are the augmentation of the technological, a supplement to the original.

46. Kelly writes, "We are not the same folks who marched out of Africa. Our genes have coevolved with our inventions...Technology has domesticated us. As fast as we remake our tools, we remake ourselves. We are coevolving with our technology, and so we have become deeply dependent on it...We are now symbiotic with technology." Kevin Kelly, *What Technology Wants* (New York: Viking, 2010), 37.

47. Suchman writes, "By situated actions I mean simply actions taken in the context of particular, concrete circumstances." Lucy Suchman, *Plans and Situated Actions: The Problem of Human-Machine Communication* (New York:

Cambridge University
Press, 1987), viii.
of HCI. I believe her concept of the situated applies to a
broader understanding of the mechanics of agency.

The networked subject is situated in two senses. In the
use of networked media, we have expanded the situations
in which we might act; we have more environments of
actuality even if we have fewer indices of the real. Additionally, we have the ability to increasingly engage situations
of personal agency, even if this does not translate into a
situation of total autonomy.

Situated action continues to be an important concept
for mediated human interactions in a culture where avatars,
not the AI of chatbots, are the ascendant. In thinking about
the mediated face-to-face exchange as well as looking at
qualities of the augmented reality platforms we use to make
these connections, the question of how we are situated
across networks of engagement comes to the fore.

The Networked Subject
In Jean Baudrillard's theory of the procession of simulacra
(1981), a theory he formulated before the event of mass
adoption of networked digital media, Western culture is
already lost in the haze of simulation where we mistake
the map for the territory. Baudrillard describes the procession of simulacra as a fact of the post-industrial world. And
we have seen an augmentation of mass communication
media (the context of Baudrillard's critique) with network
technologies. This augmentation draws a broader technological domain of mediation and simulation.

The critical rethinking we must do is to recognize the
different sites of engagement in which we participate as
actual. In doing so, we gain a contextual understanding of
what we do. We also gain an expanded field of engagement
in which we have the capacity to feel present to each other.
What we lose is the domain of the face-to-face encounter as
the exclusive site of engagement.

At the end of the twentieth century, the language of
new media spoke of the radical change that moving from
analog to digital reproduction produced on the multiple
plains of material production, information flows, and the

convergence of platforms. In the early twenty-first century, we reimagine the terms of agency to include networks of engagement where actions are situated across a spectrum of contexts. The contingencies of space, place, and time shift with a global network. In my analysis of the networked subject, I find the possibility of agency that is not contingent on a historical formulation of a command-control structure but on shifting ground. We are in fact defining for ourselves an "emergent interactive agency" based on the situational of our sites of engagement.

One of the strongest images for a global network comes from twentieth-century Dutch painter-architect Constant Nieuwenhuys (professionally known as Constant). His 1956 vision New Babylon projected a world literally girded with an imagined exoskeleton of interlaced networks or "megastructures." Constant envisioned a technological sublime where mediation stands as the threshold for all events. He saw himself as drafting a blue print for the utopian network society to come.

Since that moment, we have actually achieved a global informational network of cables, fiber optics, and wireless signals. We find ourselves at a stage of new media adoption in which the world can be animated at an unprecedented scale and pace. As networked subjects, we continue on in a procession of media technologies. In light of an ongoing acceleration of mediation, the question we continue to ask is whether we find a euphoric experience—the utopic as expressed by Constant—or an impenetrable haze of advanced simulation—as expressed by a theorist such as Jean Baudrillard.

If we are to understand what pervasive media means in terms of the global and its implications for the future, we need to recognize the increasingly shared space of the actual. In a network society where media technologies have gained ubiquity, the media augmentation does not represent a space apart from lived experience; it represents an informational layer in continuum with the physical world. In my understanding of networked media and its technical affordances, I see a critical moment to look again at how agency is configured in a network age.

The God Crosses Over: Media Adoption and Cultural Change
Like the concepts of virtuality and simulation, avatars long precede computer-mediated communications. Avatar is essentially a verb: *ava*, meaning "down," and, *tarati*, indicating the "base of." In Sanskrit, the language of origin, "avatar" held the basic meaning of "descent," lending the word spiritual meaning; "the god crosses over." In Hindu mythology, avatar originally indicated an action taken by a deity to incarnate in earthly form as animal or human. For example, the god Vishnu in avatar form may appear as the human heroes Rama or Krishna. The word entered the English language toward the end of the eighteenth century and gained a more rhetorical and less spiritual meaning. In earlier days of English usage, an avatar indicated an allegorical figure. For example, to say "she is the face of innocence" captures the sense of someone *personifying* or *embodying* a principle. Through its evolving uses, avatar has consistently given a face to the abstract or untouchable. The most recent use of avatar, ironically, reverses the process, bringing the earthly into a realm of mediated abstraction.

Avatars today are computer-generated figures most often used in digital games. Instead of a god descending into mortal guise, we find people mediated by a computer network represented by figures composed of animation and automation—speed and light as it were. Our history of being online presents two distinct turns in popular culture, both of which have determined the tenor and tone of media adoption. Cyberspace as pure information space, with its tacit urge to leave the corporal body behind, defines the first period of early Internet use through 1994. Visualization of information, with the desire to create additional "bodies", marks the emergence of the World Wide Web and carries us through the early years of the first millennial decade.

When the writer William Gibson first populated cyberspace in his 1980s fictions, such as *Neuromancer*,

it was Haitian voodun gods who were the lords of the information ether. Oshun, Elegba, and other spirits traveled
the crossroads between worlds, sharing the space only
with hackers—those who made their business the command of digital networks. The world of information be-
longed to an elite composed of a pantheon of actual gods
and an ascendant one. The magic of *logos*—word, light,
and spirit—rendered into code becomes the illuminated
text of the Internet.[48]

In the early stories of William Gibson and fellow writers
such as Vernor Vinge and Pat Cadigan, finite beings or mere
mortals gain the power of the network, weaving together
patterns of infinite reach and monumental impact. In those
early years of popular imagination fixed on virtuality, cyberspace created for many of us the kind of giant ambitions
that visions for the space age and *Star Trek* had for the
previous generation.

Between the original *Star Wars* film trilogy and the
cyber genre of science fiction, the people who would grow
up to program applications for the Internet had already
been programmed themselves with a distinct cultural code.
A world of heroes as hackers, Jedis as Zen space cowboys,
and the super atomic bomb of the Death Star fill a generation's imagination. We see the promised means of transport
of that moment and thrill at the prospect of transmitting
ourselves through information like a god. Gibson really
never told us what "cyberspace" looked like. Rather than
creating a world of simulation that mimicked the world we
knew, he left it up to our imagination to fill in the blanks
or wonder at the vastness of the territory.

The World Wide Web (1991) stimulated a profound
change in Internet use; it made information more graphical and it made network communication ultimately easier
for more people. The web brought to the Internet, over
time, customized sites, ecommerce, search engines, social
networks, blogs, wikis, and video sharing. The great disse-
mination of networked media had begun. This more graphical
and more popular Internet provides the immediate background for the current development of visual, mobile, and

48. In this case it is
magic along the lines
of Arthur C. Clarke, the
lion of twentieth-
century science fiction,
wherein "any technol-
ogy sufficiently new
presents itself as
magic," as opposed to
the young wizards of
Hogwarts variety.

pervasive media use. It is the backdrop to the emergence
of X-reality practices that link the virtual and real.

In 1994, three years after the launch of the web, a
little known writer named Neal Stephenson coined the
term "meta-verse" in his novel *Snow Crash* to describe a
graphically rich virtual reality. *Snow Crash* makes clear
the potential of avatars as reliable proxies for mediated
face-to-face engagements. Stephenson describes a world
in which computergenerated figures interact on a purely
simulated plane as liaisons for their users. Actual meetings would be held in virtual smoke filled bars with code
daemons playing the role of club bouncers that would au-
tomate the business of throwing out the trash, otherwise
known as unruly participants.

In Stephenson's vision, all of the fantastic visual representation of human exchange was based upon the magic
of code: the tendril of smoke wafting between avatars and
the delicately nuanced facial expression of each avatar are
the result of computational processes so elegantly automated
that an avatar felt like a second skin. Here was a world of
computer simulation that impacted our waking life. If avatars did not have to be visually rich to inhabit cyberspace,
they now had to be so for the metaverse.

Stephenson's invention of the metaverse essentially
narrates the confluence of change in computer graphic
imaging and Internet adoption of the time and became the
second iconic turn in popular culture depictions of informational networks. The metaverse is not an online graphically
rich virtual reality; rather, it describes a crossroads of
modalities of mediation and presence, i.e., a crossroads
of networked realities. Mirror worlds, virtual worlds,
augmented reality, and lifelogging compose the cross-
functioning sectors of worlds virtual, real and in between.

Technology designer Alan Kay, a pioneer in graphical
user interface, provided an epigram for new media adoption in 1978 that holds equally true now: any new technology
today becomes culture for the next generation. We have
rendered the Internet common and, according to Kay's
theory, this provides the strongest sign of media adoption

and reflexive social change. Media theorist Clay Shirky advances that line of thought by arguing that it is only when a technology becomes quotidian that it becomes culturally interesting.[49] Fundamentally the Internet no longer belongs to an elite set. It belongs to all of us. The current change toward visual, mobile, and pervasive media use is based on this genealogy of the avatar: from disembodied to graphically represented, from the exclusive to the popular. This continuum in popular imagination and media design forms the backdrop to the emergence of X-reality practices that link the virtual and real.

49. Clay Shirky, *Here Comes Everybody: The Power of Organizing Without Organizations* (New York: Penguin, 2008).

Jumping Through the Skylight
Sitting in Building Seven writing this passage as the afternoon sun streams across the marble floor, I glimpse up at the skylight at the top of the iconic MIT dome in Cambridge, alongside the Charles river. I can't shake the feeling that I have jumped through that same skylight. One night, some months before, I stopped by the MIT Island in Second Life, which contains a virtual Building Seven, or, a 3D model of the landmark. I found the place desolate, which was not unusual. I played with the media screens embedded in the Kresge Court lawn simulation for a bit as I thought about my meeting with the machinima group scheduled to take place on this site the following week. Then I walked into the lobby and found an Easter egg, an unmarked surprise built into the simulation. On the floor, I did not find the elegant marble pattern of the real room but, instead, a colorful bull's-eye set in the center. When I stepped on it, I bounced up as if on a trampoline. After gaining momentum, I vaulted myself all the way to the ceiling only to suddenly pop through the roof. To my surprise, I found myself sitting on top of the dome, overlooking the student construction and dock area of the island (see figure 1.7).

I roused myself from this reverie and looked back at the computer screen before me as I tried to make sense of what had just happened. I can remember recalling movie scenes or pieces of novels or comic books that appeared so vividly that I felt, in some way, as if the story told were part

Hailing frequency: The author's avatar,
Cute Robot, waving from Second Life.
Credit: B. Coleman

Fig.1.7

of my actual story. But I found this to be a different quality of recollection entirely; it felt physical. And, it felt real. I flashed back on recent neuroscience research on mirror neurons that described a cessation of pain in an amputated limb (a phantom pain) when the patient saw the limb mirrored in a looking glass.[50] A virtual image helped to reconcile actual pain even if the pain was not physiologically grounded. Perhaps the mapping I experienced, where the real space overlapped with the virtual, lay outside of more familiar mediated experiences, such as reading or watching a movie.

We can find a strong sense of identification, even overlap, between the real and the simulated. We can also experience an unnerving vertigo in the places of distortion and difference between what we know to be real and what we have actually experienced in the virtual. We have learned from Alice's adventures through the looking glass and other tales of fantastic transformation that mirrors can do very funny things. In addition to reflecting, they can also act as portals, leading to something else. If we dutifully follow the stories, we know that one of the consequences of falling down such rabbit holes is that the world we return to never looks quite the same again.

Media use, as technohumanists Norbert Wiener and Marshall McLuhan have argued, changes the user. With each shift in automation, simulation, and transmission, we discover not only new technologies but also new facets of ourselves. In other words, our modes of communication impact our concepts of space, place, and time; as we change modalities of representation, we also change our human perspective. The trend in media design over the past two decades has been a progressive movement toward synchronous communications beyond the medium of telephony. We may now include visual signals and paralinguistic gestures in our mediated communications. It becomes increasingly apparent that over the next decade we will see a greater amplification of such real-time processes. Virtual gatherings, such as Lawrence Lessig's book reading, illustrate where we have arrived in the early years of the twenty-first century with

50. In the neuroscience fields, mirror neurons are a fairly new discovery that suggest our minds map onto our bodies not only experiences we have ourselves but experiences we have seen with others. For example, neurophysiologists Giacomo Rizzolatti in his groundbreaking work on mirror neurons observed similar brain response in macaque monkeys when the monkey would reach for food and when the monkey observed others reaching for food. In behavioral neurology, V. S. Ramachandran discusses the link between mirror neurons and phenomenon as diverse as phantom pain and imitation learning. He suggests that the ability in the brain to virtually model behavior has been crucial to human evolution. For a preliminary set of citations, see Giacomo Rizzolatti, "The Mirror Neuron System and its Function in Humans," *Anatomy and Embryology* 210, no. 5-6 (October 2005): 419-421; V. S. Ramachandran and William Hirstein, "The perception of phantom limbs," *Brain* 121 (1998): 1603-1630.

51. Howard Rheingold,
"A Slice of Life in My
Virtual Community,"
In Global Networks:
Computers and Inter-
national Communica-
tion, ed. Linda M.
Harasim (Cambridge,
MA: MIT Press, 1993),
57-80.

simulation as an increasingly regular aspect of our daily lives. As networked subjects we desire more, not less, contact. And, we like to have multiple channels through which we can send our message. We feel the global power of these connections. The real effects in the world, such as political mobilization or friendship bonds, reinforce the power of identity located in the networks we create.

Online community pioneer and virtual reality explorer Howard Rheingold wrote in 1995, "The most important clues to the shape of the future at this point might not be found in looking more closely at the properties of silicon, but in paying attention to the ways people need to, fail to, and try to communicate with one another."[51] His words hold true today. Human communication among human beings still calls for greater understanding, particularly in light of the proliferation of media channels.

Cory Doctorow: Networked Persona

What follows is an interview with Cory Doctorow, writer and champion blogger. Author of many well-known speculative fiction novels, including *Big Brother*, *Makers*, and *For the Win*, he is also a coeditor of Boingboing.net, one of the most widely read blogs on the Internet. In the interview, Doctorow discusses his media consumption, outsourcing strategies, and virtually sustained relationships. Doctorow's networked media practice is essentially a social practice. And, I would suggest that he illuminates key concepts of de Certeau's "everyday" for a networked generation. At the time of the interview Doctorow was a teaching fellow at the Annenberg School for Information.

Location: Annenberg School for Information, University of Southern California, May 15, 2007

DOCTOROW: I get up at 5:00, water the plants, put the bird seed out, and then I go into the office and I sit down in front of the computer. And the first thing I do, is I go through all my email, and I delete all the SPAM and answer anything that takes, like, less than twenty seconds to answer, anything that's a one-word answer. While that's happening, I load up my tabs [URLs], group of a couple hundred tabs. And then, I start looking at RSS [real simple syndication] items, while the tab group is loading, adding tabs to it. And then, I go through all the blog suggestions and load up any of those that look interesting. And then, I go through all the items I've opened and all the blogs suggestions in a row—through hundreds of tabs, leaving me with these five tabs or five things to blog. And this whole time I'm usually listening to music from my playlist. Any time I'm walking anywhere, like even if I get up for lunch and walk into the bathroom, I'll put my iPod in and listen to a few seconds of podcast. ...I open every class by giving away books to my students.

INTERVIEWER: How nice.

DOCTOROW: As part of my media consumption I give my mail to my students. I got an N800 Nokia tablet and a Chumby the other day. It's a really cool little device. I took those up to my students, and said, every week, I'm going to give you these things, and I'm going to ask you to find something interesting to do with it and come back and present for five minutes next week.

INTERVIEWER: Right.

DOCTOROW: I spent a lot of time shoulder surfing Alice [Taylor, at the time Vice President of Digital Media, BBC, and Doctorow's soon-to-be wife] while she's playing and asking her dumb questions about WoW [World of Warcraft], and about all the Xbox titles and everything else. I don't play. I just...there is nowhere in my life to put play, but like I outsource some of my media consumption to my students. I outsource my gaming to Alice. And so, I watch her play.

INTERVIEWER: Outside of that primary relationship with Alice, in your adult life with your friends, what is the difference between being virtually social and physically social?

DOCTOROW: My peer group and I are almost only virtual, right. I have almost no physical contact with my peers. And when I do, it's usually while traveling. I sometimes will have a day at Disneyland with my friends and that's a very physically social activity.... I subscribe to game designer Raph Koster's idea that the point of most games is to figure out what the point of the game is. And I think that is true of Second Life [SL], too. That many SL players treat the big game of SL as figuring out what game they should play in SL. So, lately I've been feeling very nostalgic for a time in my life when I would go to summer camp every summer. At the summer camp, I would spend a lot of time sitting out in a hammock by the lake. And I don't do anything like that anymore. I don't know that there is any activity like that using computers or the Internet. And it's the only thing I can think of that isn't trying to figure out what game to play, is the sitting alone by yourself, reflecting in a hammock.

Putting a Face on Things

The Virtual Is Older than Simulation

Historian and theorist of modern media culture Anne Friedberg, in her discussion of virtuality from the age of perspective painting to the current period of computer-mediated simulation, makes the key point that how we see changes who we are (how we see ourselves). It is often technological innovations in the visual field that stimulate this change. Freidberg argues that through our manipulation of media—the applied mathematics of perspective painting as she discusses—we perceive the world differently.

She gives the example of Leon Battista Alberti, who in his 1435 treatise on painting and perspective, *De Pictura*, became the first to articulate the transfer of the three-dimensional world to a two-dimensional plane.[1] Alberti perceived the world differently, as something that could be made schematic and virtually rendered. That difference comes to be reflected back in how we understand ourselves; we begin to see in the physical world around us geometric order and points of harmony that previously had only appeared as disordered acts of nature: the harmoniously ordered world of Renaissance paintings

1. Anne Friedberg, *The Virtual Window* (Cambridge, MA: MIT Press, 2008), 1.

reflected the aspirations of the philosophy and technology
of the time.

From the Renaissance to the present, Friedberg states
of the history of visual simulation: "Virtual images transformed the twentieth century understanding of reality."[2]
I cite Friedberg's argument for her insight that a technical
change of perspective can stimulate changes in human
perception. She relates the mechanics of vision and visualization with the idea that the world is always a construction as such (the virtual in her language). For the current
generation, a networked one, we find a revivification of
the visual and perceptual. In effect, we are putting a face
on things. In this chapter I discuss the visual history of
avatars before they became embodied figures. I also describe a model of cognitive perception of mediated images
from experimental research. I put into relation discourses
of technical design, cultural comprehension, and a science
of perception.

Emoticon Rising
In the 1980s, an era of dial-up modems and expensive
connectivity, real-time text chat represented state of the
art. For most computer users until 1991, almost the entire
Internet was text-based, but that did not mean users lacked
expressive graphical means (1991 hailed the launching of
the World Wide Web and emergence of general image com-
pression codecs such as jpeg). For a long time, emoticons,
the graphical manipulation of regular punctuation, were
the primary use of "avatars" in everyday computing.

;-)

If you, dear reader, have never before seen an image like this except as absurd punctuation, please cock
your head to the left and you will see the icon represents
a winking smiley face. Or, consider (n_n), which is the
Japanese emoticon for smiley face. The emoticons indicate a human emotion, a smile, assembled from punctuation marks. In this vein, computer text graphically

conveys human sentiment; one also finds along this line computer art made of ASCII code. In both cases, we find code (of different orders) enlisted in the work of human communication by simulating images. We can read these images because we have the ability to create meaning around abstraction, i.e., we have a terrific drive for image making, image decoding, and, as I discuss below, attributing personality to the inanimate. In effect, with emoticons, we are making faces out of things in a manner that hails a long history of iconicity. Media theorist Florian Cramer writes of an irrepressible human urge to create icons:

> Emblems, allegorical images, were hugely popular in the Renaissance since Italian humanist scholar Andreas Alciatus published the first emblem book in 1531. Just as desktop icons on computer operating systems were invented in the 1970s in the Xerox PARC labs in order to simplify interaction with the computer as a machine performing formal-logical manipulations of coded symbols, emblems served to simplify and popularize interaction with religious and philosophical meaning.[3]

As Cramer argues, making emblems or icons traditionally makes something complex easier to decipher.[4] In addition to the human interest in making something complex simpler, I see a human interest in conveying emotion. The iconic and the graphic, in my estimation, have continuously been enlisted in making our relation to media and our mediated relations between each other more social. We mark our things with faces or other forms of proprietary markers to customize them in such a way that they feel habitable. If we apply this logic to pervasive media, we now have a broadly expanded territory we might call home.

From Text to Animation: Avatars as Figures of Transition
Virtual worlds describe one such expansion of evocative, communicative space we have inhabited with emoticons, icons, and images on the road to pervasive media engagement.

3. Florian Cramer, *Words Made Flesh* (Rotterdam: Piet Zwart Institute, 2004), 23.

4. Coinciding with the innovation in computer graphics over the past two decades, user interface (UI) designers have developed many kinds of graphical interface structures. In 1985, Apple Inc. (then Apple Computer) changed the tenor of popular computing with the creation of an operating system that used icons, such as images of folders and files, instead of the standard text-based DOS system.

The history of computer-simulated virtual worlds is essentially as long as the history of computing. The worlds span the most basic text exchanges to the most complex of graphical and procedural simulations. A virtual world exists on a computer server or a series of servers configured to allow many people to access the same information at the same time. The virtual worlds allow real-time interactions among the players. This means we can have synchronous conversations and direct feedback. Built of computer code, a virtual world presents persistent information to players about where they are, what is happening, and what it looks like.

Text-based virtual worlds are more than twenty years old now. For text-based worlds, visualization takes place in the imagination, as one must read through descriptions of fellow players and context. In graphical worlds, the computer network generates an image that everyone can see. Additionally, when I add something to the world—a new room to a dungeon or a red hat on my avatar's head—everyone can see that virtual object as well.

The first text-based multiuser dungeon (MUD) lived on the intranet at Essex University beginning in 1979. Graphically simulated virtual worlds appeared in nascent form as early as 1985. The rich graphical and interactive experience we have now in networked virtual worlds arose in the 2000s with the dawn of the massively multiplayer online game (MMOG) and the accessible price of processing power. The primary difference between text-based and graphical worlds is that graphical worlds present dimensionality. There is a virtual embodiment that adds shared perceptual experiences of visualized objects, motion, and directionality. Not only can we see (and sometimes create) images that live in the world, but also the images are animated, they have depth, and they adhere to "physics." For example, when I drop something in a text-based world, a line of code appears announcing to all that "Player X has dropped the cup." When I drop something in a graphical world you see it leave my hands and hit the floor. The same terms of shared sensory perception go for the experience of navigating a graphical space. Instead of text that narrates my actions, you see an avatar walk up and down the steps to the castle. Additionally, I can have a face, a body, and gestures in the form of the avatar.

The importance of putting a "face" to networked communication plays itself out along several lines of technical development, information visualization, and human communication interests. I relate in the following section the history of twenty years of virtual world design in order to point out that this is not the first time we have had a go at networked worlds. However, these spaces have combined with several other factors to make graphical real-time multiuser spaces not new but *newly important.*

We see at this time a shift in real-time communication media that we have not witnessed since the advent of the telephone. I discuss here two phases of virtual world development and use in order to decode what is happening currently in pervasive networked media. The first period I discuss, which includes text-based worlds as well as the early graphical ones, essentially spans 1979 through 1991, when the World Wide Web launched. The second period I address, 1995 to the present, includes the major innovations in graphical web. In phase one, we see primarily design, use, and adoption of real-time multiuser platforms among researchers and niche communities. In phase two, the technical changes as well as the cultural changes in network use have created a context for an emergent popular adoption of virtual world platforms.

Walled Gardens and Other Rare Flowers
In 1979, one of the nascent characteristics of early virtual worlds was that they functioned essentially as closed universes. To visit was to take a vacation from the real world and enter a walled garden. A walled garden describes both a fantasyland where real-world rules and consequences do not come into play and a hermetic space that is not influenced by external factors. For example, writer C. S. Lewis's character Lucy may be a princess in the kingdom of Narnia, but she remains just a little girl on the other side

5. Bartle, *Interactive Multi-User Computer Games*, technical report, BT Martlesham Research Laboratories, Dec. 1990. <http://www.mud.co.uk/richard/imucg.htm>.

of the magic wardrobe, in real life. Historically as a society, we have found a great many valuable uses for walled garden experiences, particularly for children. They often create the space for us to explore new roles (a reigning princess as opposed to a powerless little girl), even as they offer a safety net of little or no consequence for our actions.

We have begun to exchange closed worlds for open, and walled gardens for porous nets. In the past thirty-some years, I see an evolution in virtual worlds away from insular experiences and toward persistent networked relationships. That evolution plays out in the design of applications as well as in the engagement of platforms.

In their early text-based period, virtual worlds had to be found, usually by word of mouth through a friend. You had to get on the network. And, you had to deal with often glitchy code and imperfect design (not everything has changed since 1979). A self-selecting group, often composed of the same young computer scientists who worked on the university network during the day found their way into electric dungeons at night.[5] MUD1 (multiuser dungeon) written by Roy Trubshaw and Richard Bartle of Essex University on a DECsystem-10 mainframe, trail blazed the genre and remains to this day one of the most famous applications of text-based adventure games. The popularity of *Colossal Cave* followed by *Zork*, single-player computerized adventures, inspired Trubshaw and Bartle to create the code for MUD. Their innovation of the multiuser format changed online game history.

To begin with, only Essex students on the university intranet could access MUD1. A year after its debut, word had spread and outside players began accessing the game by calling into networked modems from their homes. MIT computer scientist Hal Abelson describes coming home one evening to find his eleven-year-old daughter calling into the network modem of the MIT Computer Science and Artificial Intelligence Lab (where he worked) to access the MUD. (In the early 1980s, the password RMS, the initials of Richard Stallman, the initiating author of GNU code and the Free Software movement, got you onto the system.

The password for the network paid homage to Abelson's student Stallman, just as Abelson's work in object-oriented programming languages became part of the inspiration for two game designers who would make the first graphical multiuser game, Habitat.) After a few weeks of obsessive play, Abelson's daughter was running her own dungeon.[6] The talents needed to run a multiuser dungeon reside with two kinds of writing. On the design end, one needs the ability to work within the "framework of discrete [code] objects," as Bartle describes it, that create the technical workings of the game.[7] On the user end, the part that the players see, one needs to be able to vividly describe a world. Literally, players would navigate through mazes of text that described environment, objects, and other players. Bartle underscores the importance of good writing for MUD game design: "For text-based [Multi-User Adventures]...the impact of well-written room and object descriptions on new players cannot be underestimated."[8] In the two layers of "code" that create MUD1, I draw attention to a pattern that will come fully into use in the development of networked media from those early days to the present: the technical platform remains essentially open and the participants design the particular use of the space, place, and temporality of engagement. The marking as habitat, whether in language or graphical image, becomes an important pre-cedent for how we have entered an age of avatars.

Age of Avatars

Avatars and their virtual worlds have tweaked the curiosity of the generation that came of age with the a graphical Internet, i.e., the web. By the spring of 2008 there were an estimated thirty-five million people playing in virtual worlds in North American and European territories.[9] An estimated 150 million played worldwide.[10] World of Warcraft, a game world, accounts for about eleven million paid subscriptions of that number.[11] Second Life, a social world, reported seven million visitors to the platform. The saturation numbers in South Korea for Cyworld, a 2D Web and mobile virtual world, were 40 percent of the population,

6. Hal Abelson, personal interview, May 16, 2007.

7. Bartle, *Interactive Multi-User Computer Games*, 17.

8. Ibid., 25.

9. The Virtual World News, an online periodical that chronicles business news on virtual worlds reported these numbers in 2008, posting to <http://www.virtualworldnews.com>. The group subsequently renamed itself Engage Digital and redirected its content to <http://www.engagedigital.com>.

10. George Jobi, "Virtual Worlds: The Story of Two Waves, 2.5D vs. 3D," October 28, 2008, <http://origin-software.intel.com/en-us/blogs/2008/10/28/virtual-worlds-the-story-of-two-waves-25d-vs-3d/>.

11. Blizzard Entertainment press release, October 28, 2008.

with twenty million unique users monthly. Why has there been such a proliferation in these platforms over the past five years? What is the value of avatars to network culture? Or perhaps let's begin with an even more basic question. What are these things?

The tipping point for an age of avatars came in 2005, which saw a proliferation of graphical virtual platforms designed for all kinds of activity: social worlds, medical training worlds, business worlds, kids' worlds, and game worlds. These were commercially produced virtual worlds designed for general users. Influential companies such as IBM, Disney, Google, and Viacom created branded multiuser spaces that played with new ways of expanding the experience of the Magic Kingdom or MTV. First out in 1999, well in advance of the trend, Viacom's Webkinz world connected virtual play with real-world stuffed animals. Instead of an imaginary space where stuffed animals could talk to children, players had an actual shared virtual space where that happened.

Disney opened a popular Magic Kingdom virtual world to celebrate the anniversary of the theme parks (the parks when created in the 1950s were already a type of virtual world of their own). The enthusiasm for the virtual forum was such that when Disney chose to shut down the virtual Magic Kingdom after it had run its course, the players staged a protest to keep it open. Disney extended its virtual world holdings in 2005 when it acquired Club Penguin, a youth-oriented virtual world populated by penguin avatars, developed by a Canadian media design group. With its combination of causal games, customizability, and group activities, Club Penguin has proven to be one of the most popular and lasting virtual worlds. Internationally, Korea, Finland, Japan, and China all have major offerings in the virtual worlds. From Japan, the Hello Kitty virtual world came online in 2007. Habbo Hotel, the Finnish-server young adult world, became the first virtual world with its own Hollywood agent in 2008.

In terms of avatars and virtual worlds in a narrow sense, particularly in Western countries, children and young adults adopted them in great numbers and ease. For adults it remained largely an alien technology, used by people on the fringe of the culture. As I describe in looking at the Second Life hype cycle (see chapter 1), the media coverage of virtual world properties subsided after this three year period (2005–2008) of explosive growth and attention. We find in 2011 a virtual world landscape described by robust participation in fantasy, fighting, and other game worlds and expansive growth in what I describe as another kind of avatar engagement: social media such as profile pages, VoIP, IM, and SMS. In effect, we practiced in the early years of avatar adoption how a broader adoption of pervasive media might work.

3D Web

Whether you know it or not—and most people have had little reason to pay attention—the 3D web made a strong showing in 1998. The 3D web indicates a shift from a text-based Internet to a graphical one, and one that is three-dimensional in terms of how information is configured. We do not yet have a fully functional 3D web, and it remains debatable whether we would truly desire to have a majority of our interactions augmented with dimensionality. Nonetheless, in 1998, when the second international Virtual Worlds conference of computer scientists and media designers met in Paris, the discussion focused on engaging the social aspect of network relations as a newfound power as well as on the graphical explosion in interactive design. In a sense, everything that we see currently from 3D animated avatars to persistent virtual worlds was test driven a decade ago.

By the time of the Paris conference several commercial virtual world platforms existed in addition to the ones designed for research purposes. AlphaWorld, The Palace, Onlive!, all had opened up shop for public use with 3D interface and avatars.[12] Business schools published papers mentioning Blaxxun Interactive's Community as a rich model for real-world training. Sony's Community Place foreshadowed by a decade its recent PlayStation-console virtual world

12. Bruce Damer, *Avatars!* (Chicago: New Light, 1998).

13. Frédéric Kaplan,
Angus McIntyre,
Chisato Numaoka, and
Silvère Tajan, "Growing
Virtual Communities
in 3D Meeting Spaces,"
in J. C. Heudin (ed.):
Virtual Worlds 98,
LNAI 1434, 1998, 286.

called *Home*. Computer scientists and segments of industry lobbied hard with media producers and the public to adopt VRML (virtual reality markup language) and universal standards for 3D imaging.

At the 1998 conference, four computer scientists delivered a paper entitled "Growing Virtual Communities in 3D Meeting Spaces" in which they state:

> This new understanding of the Internet as a social medium constitutes a basic assumption for many developers of browsers for 3D virtual worlds. Environments such as Blaxxun Interactive's Community, Cryo's Deuxiéme Monde, OnLive! Technologies' Traveller, and Sony's Community Place are all based on a similar model—*a more or less realistic visual world in which people meet to socialize* [emphasis mine].[13]

Who reading this currently has an active account with Community Place or Deuxiéme Monde? In regard to those pioneering 3D interactive worlds, the problem with sustainability echoes the problem with new media adoption. Historically, "new" fails to be popular until it becomes old enough for people to fathom. "Old enough" means a new technology has been sufficiently vetted by the early adopters and the hobbyists; and then the rest of us join in *if* there is sufficient motivation, which persists as a powerful caveat.

Two coinciding factors prepare the stage for the emergence of pervasive media as social media engagement: the arrival of immersive platforms, such as massively multiplayer online games (MMOs or MMOGs), and increasingly rich-media social network platforms, such as Flickr (the photo sharing site). Online multiuser video games advanced the technology for graphical avatar-based play so profoundly that by 2004 millions of gamers had essentially trained for more expansive uses of navigable 3D space. In parallel, we have used social media platforms to practice ever increasing degrees of connectivity. For example, the unprecedented massive use of a multimedia social network site such as Facebook builds on these combined histories of networked media.

In regard to MMOGs, in the span of a few years, with the emergence of multiplayer platforms and the increased accessibility of broadband Internet in developed countries, we stumbled upon an entirely changed landscape. Ultima Online (Origin Systems/Electronic Arts), a multiplayer fantasy game or role-playing game (RPG), did not invent the genre in 1997, but it did change the game, becoming the first "massively" played networked game with hundreds of thousands of players at its peak. Everquest, the 1999 Sony/Verant interactive MMO offering, became fondly known as "evercrack." It broke the mold not only in player numbers but also in player addiction, the strong feelings around the games and the communities of friends developed in the play across DSL lines.

From the point of view of popular culture, what we saw of MMOs at the end of the 1990s still constituted "fringe" engagement; despite growing numbers, gamers continued to be viewed as shut-ins and social outcasts.[14] Yet what did not become obvious until nearly a decade later was the change in the network engagement that the MMO gamers were beta testing for the rest of us. In a big way, interactive dimensional space had opened up for network users outside of niche-use groups.

The hobbyists and enthusiastic computer scientists of 1998 can say they were right about the potential of these virtual spaces. They just got the timeframe and the technology wrong. The graphical online world of that period was made up of objects and operations still too ugly, too difficult, and simply too nerdy to have broad appeal. As for VRML, fate did not deal it a winner's hand. The seismic flux in mediation that HTML (hypertext markup language) had created in 1991 regarding the adoption of the World Wide Web fizzled later in the decade with the would-be visual companion to the Internet protocol. I asked a respected computer scientist active during that period why VRML did not fly. He replied simply, "It was too hard."

14. T. L. Talyor, *Play between Worlds: Exploring Online Game Culture* (Cambridge, MA: MIT Press 2006).

15. Media theorist Friedrich Kittler, who analyzes the social history of technical media, says we err greatly on the side of the anthropomorphic relation to technology, particularly in the American ethos. He suggests that in finding human narratives for machines we miss the ways in which machines affect human narrative. See John Armitage, "From Discourse Networks to Cultural Mathematics: An Interview with Friedrich A. Kittler," *Theory, Culture & Society* 23, 2006 (7–8): 28.

Designing Media

The research on embodied agents of the 1990s takes very seriously the question, what does "adding a face" mean for human use of computers? In this moment in the early twenty-first century, we shift our focus from human-computer relations to human-to-human mediated relations, the C3 interaction of communication, community, and collaboration. In looking at the legacy of avatars, we find embodiment agents driven by *users* not by computers. Developing AI no longer provides the goal for the design strategy, but rather something more old-fashioned yet diabolically complex: human-to-human communication... at a distance.

The line I am drawing takes us from the very earliest text-based graphics, such as emoticons or ASCII art, through the automation of agents to the user-manipulated 3D avatars we find today. The technology that facilitates each level of representation differs, but the urge to create an image that imparts basic human emotions in mediated communication remains consistent. The anthropomorphic drive to create a likeness, to find the familiar, may very well make us feel more at home, but it can also cover over important information about what we are doing in the course of mediation and how we are doing it.[15] We have added image and animation channels to what had previously been audio only. Does this make for better communication? Not necessarily; more information is not always better. Does it make for rich new combinations of information? Yes.

Media use, as media theorists from Norbert Wiener to Marshall McLuhan have argued, changes the user. With each shift and often each increase in automation, simulation, and transmission, we discover not only new technologies but new ways by which we extend our presence. I have suggested that the direction in media design over the past three decades to create increased visualization brings up new questions about how we engage media and, specifically, networked forms. If we have an anthropomorphic urge to humanize our things with faces, what are the consequences of a pervasive media engagement where we stay present to each other via real-time and often visual simulation? As we change modalities of mediation, in what ways do we also change our "human" perspective?

The Media Equation: The Computational Persona
X-reality, a continuum of experience across real and simulated sites, is not necessarily a new phenomenon if we look at issues of perception. When it comes to media use, Stanford professors Byron Reeves and Clifford Nass say that we have always blended the virtual and the real. In our minds we blend signals from the living and the animated. We grant animated forms—things that give the appearance of being alive or humanlike—agency. In effect, we cannot distinguish between real and simulated signals.

In the 1980s, inspired by the fast-emerging world of personal computers and the networks that linked them, and after nearly forty years in communication research, Reeves framed the question: How do people react to a mediated image? To answer this question, Reeves and colleague Nass, a research scientist focusing on communication and computers, designed a series of laboratory experiments to assess how subjects responded to traditional forms of media—like television—as well as the new media simulations of computers. In what became the groundbreaking findings, they discovered that people cannot perceive a difference between a mediated image and a real person or object before them.

In the fields of psychology and communication, one can find a great deal of research on the impact of media on people—behaviorally, culturally, and emotionally, particularly in childhood development. In technical and design fields of media, studies abound on how users behave and what they like. Nass and Reeves were the first to ask seriously and systematically about the ways in which this new media is perceived not as content or culture but as phenomenon. In the literature across the fields of communication, HCI, and psychology, this phenomenon has come to be known, after the research by Reeves and Nass, as the media equation.

16. Byron Reeves and
Clifford Nass, *The
Media Equation: How
People Treat Computers,
Television, and New
Media Like Real People
and Places* (Stanford:
Center for the Study of
Language and Informa-
tion, 2003).

17. Developing the
media equation thesis
in regard to current
networked engage-
ment communication
scholar Kwan Min Lee
writes: "Modern media,
computers, and simula-
tion technologies defy
the adaptive value of
rapid application of the
causal reasoning mod-
ules to all incoming
stimuli. *[P]eople keep
using their old brains—
i.e., causal reasoning
modules—when they
respond to mediated or
simulated objects*" (em-
phasis added). Kwan
Min Lee, "Why Presence
Occurs: Evolutionary
Psychology, Media
Equation, and Pres-
ence," *Presence* 13, no. 4
(August 2004): 499.

In my analysis of networked media engagement, research such as the media equation helps to illuminate our actual new media use. Because of our increasing use of computational and interactive formats, how media affects us—or how we find media affective—gains increasing importance to understanding our world, designing for it, and acting in it. For my purposes, in understanding a generational shift toward an accelerated mediation, where we engage avatars and other forms of media simulation on a nearly daily basis, I am suggesting that the media equation has strong implications for how we understand mediated presence and networked agency.

I look at the implications of these findings for a networked generation and issues around X-reality use and design. Reeves and Nass summarize the their findings in *The Media Equation*, citing over two decades of experimental research to prove their hypothesis.[16] They argue that humans suffer a cognitive lapse in reacting to empirical stimulus (activity in the world) and synthetic stimulus (the simulated activity): we perceive them to be the same.

If the media equation rings false—or at least tinny to the ear—that is because it is counterintuitive. We have all had the experience of successfully distinguishing between a character we saw in a movie and the person we see across the dinner table. And, certainly, experience, intelligence, and other factors help us negotiate the difference between real and simulated events. But, on the level of perception, Reeves and Nass explain that we are still prehistoric brains reacting in a fight or flight manner to what is before us. The reptile part of the brain did not evolve special sensors for video games; we respond to stimulus in a manner that keeps us safe in a dangerous world, and not necessarily for the purpose of blowing up digital asteroids on a screen.[17] As it turns out though, our brains are good at that too.

In regard to pervasive media, such experimental research supports my analysis of the different forms of networked presence we manifest—particularly for the real-time and visualized human signal. If we already animate with our imagination the mechanical or the simulated, we now have the experience of making actual our human presence via computational and synthetic transmission.

Of course, not all animated forms are created equal in our perception or our treatment. As I have previously discussed, we tend to get fed up very quickly with machines that impersonate people (see chapter 1). On the one hand, we are good readers of the difference between human and nonhuman signals (semantic communication), i.e., the conversation with a person versus one with a chatbot; the limits of the machinic conversation are, for the most part, easy to discern. On the other hand, simulation, when derived from human gesture, works very powerfully. For example, the recording of a baby crying can elicit the same feelings of anxiety in the listener as hearing an actual baby cry. As Reeves and Nass describe with the media equation, the distinction between a real and simulated signal proves very difficult to discern. Their findings in experimental research correspond with my analysis of networked media engagement: whether it is live or mediated, a human signal provokes a human response. (See figure 2.1.)

In a time of accelerated simulation such as ours, I ask what are the implications of the media equation. If our use of avatars is deeper and broader than ever before, if we are nearly constantly mediated, then how are we making judgments between the real and the virtual? The answer is: we are not.[18] In my analysis of the media equation, the issue at hand is not a change in technology. Rather, the primary importance of Reeves and Nass's insight relates to social rather than technical engagement of networked media.

As a species, we are largely defined by sociality. We use language, we cooperate, and we share information. All of these attributes are profoundly social ones.[19] Reeves and Nass characterize our response to media stimulus as social. Personality is the key to the media equation. "Give anything eyes and a mouth, it would seem," they write, "and personality responses follow."[20] We can describe personality as a profoundly human attribute, one that speaks to key characteristics of humanness. And yet, we grant personality

18. Reeves and Nass write, "These studies provide strong evidence for the psychological equivalence of real and mediated worlds." In effect, we perceive the real and the simulated the same; on the level of cognition, we do not make significant distinctions. *The Media Equation*, 82–83.

19. A work such as anthropologist Michael Tomasello's *Why We Cooperate* (Cambridge, MA: MIT Press, 2009) summarizes arguments and experimental literature on the subject of cooperation as an indicator of human sociality in cultural anthropology, with commentary from Carol Dweck, Joan Silk, Brian Skyrms, and Elizabeth Spelke.

20. Reeves and Nass, *The Media Equation*, 83.

Media equation: We treat images that appear on a screen as real. Image of Desire Strangelove, of the series "13 Most Beautiful Avatars." With this series artists Eva and Franco Mattes explore the visual impact of Second Life avatars. Credit: Eva and Franco Mattes, Postmasters

Fig.2.1

to things that occupy the realm of the nonhuman—the mechanical, the computational, and the synthetic. The media equation implies that we not only respond in a social manner to media technologies themselves, such as computers, but we also treat images that appear on a screen as real. In addition to these two categories, I would offer a third category of engagement that relates to pervasive media: we now create conditions in which machines augment our personality and presence.

In terms of human-machine interactions, as viewers, we fill in the blanks that turn an abstract pattern into a face or a line of text into a personality. In the 1995 paper "Can Computer Personalities Be Human Personalities?" Reeves and Nass, with additional researchers, find that it takes only the most "superficial manipulations" of a computer program to imbue it with a personality that affects the user's experience.[21] It affects us in the sense that we ascribe intention, tone, and agency to the machine. One does not need extensive graphics or natural language to create a machine with a persona.

In the experiment outlined in their article, the researchers find that even the most remedial text interaction can convey basic human expression like dominance or submission.[22] If the machine says, "Do this now!" or "Please follow this procedure," we have a very different experience of the persona of the computer, even if we understand on a logical level there is no intention behind the tone, only programming. The importance of their findings for an analysis of pervasive media is that we interpolate machines into our world as social actors.

The anthropomorphic urge is not a new one. Computer science and science fiction share a long history of machines that seem human or endowed with human persona.[23] But the shift in scale and speed of engagement with pervasive media relates to our sense of onging and intimate proximity with media objects. Both the size of media technologies, in the arrival of the handheld device, and their nearly constant physical proximity add to our social relation with technology. Our faculty of perception is not always reason-

21. Clifford Nass, Youngme Moon, B.J. Fogg, Byron Reeves, and Chris Dryer, "Can Computer Personalities Be Human Personalities?" *International Journal of Human-Computer Studies* 43, no. 2 (1995): 223–239.

22. Ibid.

23. A famous example in computer science and psychology, the ELIZA program, a text-based computer therapist program, written by Joseph Weizenbaum, had good results in working with patients based on a Rogerian psychotherapy method: the analyst primarily replies to the analysands' statements by making their words into questions, thus exploiting the best use of a computer vocabulary. ELIZA did not have to generate information or autonomous intelligence; the program simply had to be "a good listener" and reflect back what the patients told it. Despite the fact that the program did not have a human face or even a screen (it was based on printer output), Weizenbaum had designed a effective media foil for participants to fill with persona. In short, ELIZA was designed to be a good therapist.

24. Reeves and Nass,
The Media Equation, 83. able, which makes our interaction with an increasingly
animated world progressively anthropomorphic.

The second factor to keep in mind when we talk about
mediation and perception is that we not only respond in
a social manner to media appliances, we also treat images
that appear on a screen as real. As Reeves and Nass write,
"The studies show that social responses are not just applied
to the appliances that deliver media; they also apply to
fictional representations, human or otherwise, that appear
on a screen."[24] Their findings suggest that we perceive the
real world and simulated ones the same way. In people's
engagement of pervasive media (and mediation), I see this
phenomenon born out in the movement toward a societal
recognition of the actual.

We are equal opportunity agency attributors—we see
personality in almost everything, which helps to explain
the power of avatars as representatives of self. I am suggesting that the critical distinction we draw every day
is not between the real and the simulated but, rather,
between the actual (which includes trusted modes and
tropes of mediation) and the inauthentic (which describes
the kind of failed signaling produced by chatbots or other
low-level AI).

In addition to a long history of making machines
anthropomorphic and endowing media images with personality, today we have media that tethers us to other people
in real-time rich media connections. Our brains are now
juggling a new combination of factors: an unreal image that
we take to be real with an actual person managing its
motions. This happens everyday in multiplayer online games
as it happens, in different formats, on VoIP, IM, and SMS. If
we had been previously mistaken about the human capacity
of our machines and their synthesis of simulation, we now
step toward a media engagement that actually does channel
the presence of another person.

The age of computation changed the speed of transmission but not the terms of human perception. In effect, our
ancient brains are not equipped to discern real violence
from simulated violence, or any other form of simulated

signal. But this does not mean we have not changed in
rather profound ways in relation to the adoption of accelerated networked media. One can see the impact most clearly
in the dynamic forms of engagement we find within network culture. Avatars play a critical role in the next levels
of simulation and networks, as they are our messengers,
the front line of interaction.

If avatars are perceived as real, as Reeves and Nass suggest, then we take them at face value to a certain extent. Yet,
intellectually, we understand that each avatar, or the sum of
images, action, and texts that make up one's network avatar,
is a collection of media—that we are putting a face on things
in effect. I am suggesting that both sides of a media equation can be sustained: first, we believe what we see even
as we know what we see is effectively a façade; second, we
negotiation the difficulties of perception (the deception as it
may be) by gauging the located use of media. We determine
our sense of agency in pervasive media engagement in terms
of "situated action," as I have discussed in chapter 1.

The media equation thesis—that we do not perceive
a difference between the real and the simulated—has particular value for my estimation of networked subjectivity.
I am suggesting that there is no second, virtual life—
a cyberspace outside of our actual space of engagement.
Rather, there are only variations of avatars as one moves
through different territories. Actual things happen across
a continuum of space, place, and temporality. And, the
insights and actions we take in these sites may change our
minds or even our worldviews.

In my assessment of accelerated mediation on a societal scale, I see that virtual figures and territories possess
increasing capacity to affect our experience of the world.
We feel this shift in how we value and engage mediation
most deeply not in the outer reaches of media design
but in the humble media of daily life: the things we bump
into in our homes and daily travails. It is the quotidian
experience of media, not the avant garde or exceptionally
expensive, that speaks to what we actually do with media
and best forecasts the future of mediated worlds. It is within

25. Media scholar Lisa Nakamura has argued that representation of racial identity online in any format (text, visual, or a variation) is typically treated with racist hostility by a normatively white hegemonic male Internet culture. Lisa Nakamura, *Cybertypes: Race, Ethnicity, and Identity on the Internet* (New York: Routledge, 2002).

26. Paul Hemp, "Avatar-Based Marketing," *Harvard Business Review* 84, no. 6 (June 2006): 48-57.

this construct of quotidian media engagement that we must attend to issues of simulation and perception to better understand how it is we are addressing each other via mediation. Avatars are effective in conveying a human expression even if we cannot be sure who that human is.

Avatar Identity

Avatars provoke strong human responses because they send strong human signals. Taller avatars gain greater social power in their relations. Female avatars are feted and flattered or, conversely, harassed—all in greater degree than male avatars. Avatars that represent ethnicities other than white—black, Asian, Latino, and so on—often are treated by strangers in a stereotypically racist manner.[25] Gender-ambiguous avatars are treated with suspicion. Openly gay avatars get gay bashed. These social phenomena carry over from the real world into the virtual because we take our worldviews with us when we go online. If we take avatars at face value, the question becomes: To whom are we responding, the winged pixie we see animated on the screen or the person who runs her?

In a 2006 *Harvard Business Review* article written more as polemic than reportage, Paul Hemp asked that very question in querying why companies do not market to avatars.[26] "Avatar-Based Marketing," as he named the concept, would speak to our online alter egos. Hemp brought up a legitimate point. If, as the media equation suggests, we take each other's online persona as real entities, then who exactly are we addressing? Is it the player behind the screen or the synthetic figure in front of our eyes?

The answer is both, but to varying degrees. Strong identity markers, such as gender, race, and size, all carry great virtual weight online (see figure 2.2). Experimental and ethnographic research on this subject find that virtual identity markers work analogous to how they work in the real world. Avatar images, as well as gestures and voices, translate cultural information that we believe in: if we see a black avatar, we comprehend this as a black person and treat that avatar accordingly. In their paper

Visualizing networked identity:
Our engagement of avatars suggests
that markers of race, gender, sexual
orientation, and ethnicity all translate
across X-reality platforms. Image of
Nubian Craven of the series "13 Most
Beautiful Avatars." Credit: Eva and
Franco Mattes, Postmasters

Fig.2.2

27. R. Dotsch and D. H.
J. Wigboldus, "Virtual
Prejudice," *Journal of
Experimental Social
Psychology* 44, no. 4
(July 2008): 1194–1198.
See also Paul W.
Eastwick and Wendi
L. Gardner, "Is It a
Game? Evidence for
Social Influence in the
Virtual World," *Journal
of Social Influence* 4,
no. 1 (January 2009):
18–32.

"Virtual Race," Dutch psychologists Wigboldus and Dotsch ran a virtual world test where users encountered white young male avatars and Moroccan young male avatars.[27] Players had similar responses to the Moroccan avatars as they did to Moroccan young men in real life—negative in general.

For better and for worse, putting a face on things also attaches the societal associations that such a face bears. (See figure 2.3.) An obvious example is that you do not have to be female to appear in a female avatar. And, in fact, historically among networked computer gamers, it has always been that more males represent themselves with a female avatar than vice versa. When interviewed about their choice to play a female figure, male gamers give two primary reasons for doing so. The first is that they would rather look at an attractive female body while playing than a male one, even if the female body is "their own." The second standard response is that female avatars receive more courteous treatment than their male counterparts by other players. In my interviews with men using female avatars, subjects describe experiences that complicate the simple terms of male-to-female game play. If we understand that a virtual figure appears real to a viewer, then we might also look at the way in which our engagement of a virtual figure may affect our sense of self.

The more nuanced understanding of avatar identity depends on a battery of things, such as the player's sexual orientation, the nature of the game environment, and the time investment in a community and platform. Reputation over time greatly diminishes the value of appearance. On first encounter, we may act toward that virtual persona in a prescriptive way, that is, amorously, violently, and so on. Over time, as we get to know that persona, the real-world person begins to bleed across the virtual threshold. We can locate an avatar effect in which we find persuasive signs of virtual identity that are aggregated with the identity of the media participant.

An anecdote from the world of networked gamers illustrates the invitation of a virtual identity and its limits

Anthropomorphic urge: We often
create icons and images to translate human emotion across media
platforms. Image of Modesty Galbraith,
of the series "13 Most Beautiful Avatars." Credit: Eva and Franco Mattes,
Postmasters

Fig.2.3

28. SirBruce, "Confessions of an MMOG Cross-Dresser," 26 Dec 2006 8:00 am, <http://www.escapistmagazine.com/articles/view/issues/issue_77/439-Confessions-of-an-MMOG-Cross-Dresser>.

29. Ironically, when VoIP systems became prevalent in MMOs such as Halo, female players who previously had "passed" for male or at least were unmarked in terms of gender, were often harassed to the point of leaving the game when other male players heard their female voices over the line. The apparent authentication of their actual gender short-circuited the male fighter images they used on screen.

over time. A game blogger, SirBruce posted on the subject of his cross-gender exploits in "Confessions of an MMOG Cross-Dresser."[28] His saga outlines a "lesbian" relationship his female avatar had online with another female avatar, who turned out to also be a man. SirBruce describes the titillation of the lesbian romance, but does not discuss any possibility that it might also be a gay relationship between the two men. Once the relationship leaked over into their actual identities, the love affair was over. (SirBruce explains that after the avatar couple outed each other as men, they became very good friends, noting that he even hired his "buddy" for a job.)[29]

I am suggesting that avatar identity works within a space of the actual as an X-reality phenomenon. We are, in effect, neither purely role playing (pretending to be someone else), nor are we left untouched by our engagement of a persona. In keeping with the findings of the media equation, SirBruce had an experience particular to appearing female online: he was taken at face value. But the limits of his second self, his female avatar, surfaced when it came to a deepening friendship with a player. If we address the question of avatar identity, the first level of response may be to the representational persona. But to comprehend more deftly whom we are addressing, we must find a mesh of the actual—a networked portrait of an interlocutor—and speak to that identity.

Mark Lentczner: Representing Race, Sexuality, and Seeing Oneself

Mark Lentczner has a long history in virtual worlds. He began in the 1990s with his avatar Zarf in the text-based world Siberian City II. From 2005 to 2010, he was the senior systems architect at Linden Lab, the creators of the virtual world Second Life. In Second Life he was represented by two avatars, Zarf and his official Linden persona, Zero Linden. Lentczner, who identifies himself as a Caucasian, Jewish gay man, discusses in this interview his choice to use avatars of color in the graphical virtual world. He reflects on the impact of race, age, and signaling sexual orientation in a virtual community.

Location: Coffee shop, Mountain View, California, February 19, 2008

LENTCZNER: My Second Life avatar was born in June 2005. My avatar's name is Zarf Vontangerloo. Vontangerloo picked at random, as you know, from a list of possible names. I just thought, that's a cool last name. Zarf is actually a name I've used in virtual communities for decades. I was part of a virtual world environment at MIT many years ago, Siberian City II.

INTERVIEWER: Did you participate in other online worlds before you got to Second Life?

LENTCZNER: No.

INTERVIEWER: So we're talking about an almost fifteen year break.

LENTCZNER: Fast forward to 2005, and I'm a stay-at-home dad, which I loved. I had actually heard about Second Life back in its early beta period and kind of stuck it on my back burner. Well, I ran into it again. In fact, I ran into Corey [Ondrejka, the founding CTO of Linden Lab] demo'ing it at a conference. Back then, it wasn't free to be in Second Life, but they were handing out freebies. So I took their freebie code and went home. Normally I just tell people that two weeks later it was clear I was completely hooked. But since you've asked about the creation of the avatar, I'll tell you about this, because I think that is crucial.

So here's what happened in that two weeks. First I created an avatar. Zarf is modeled after, I'd say, a thirty-year-old Hawaiian mix.

INTERVIEWER: Hawaiian mix of what?

LENTCZNER: Well, he's a little Polynesian. He's a little bit Caucasian. He's somewhat a meld.

INTERVIEWER: Talk to me a little bit about Zarf not looking like you but being you. On first blush or at a distance, is Zarf often understood to be black?

LENTCZNER: No. This is an interesting question, because my business avatar is most decidedly black. Not only is my business avatar decidedly black, my business avatar is about sixty-five to seventy [years old]. I mean grey hair and balding. He's an old African-American gentleman.

INTERVIEWER: So when you're representing your company, that's the avatar you use. Let's say it's similar to using the business Blackberry, as opposed to your personal phone.

LENTCZNER: No, it's a tremendous pain in the ass.

INTERVIEWER: Procedurally it's a hassle. But let's put hassle aside, and look at the relationships you've formed. Your business avatar is an older black man. Zarf is a youngish, Polynesian male. You rez [appear] male on both parts. You rez across the spectrum of brownish to blackish.

LENTCZNER: Yes, darker than I am in real life.

INTERVIEWER: If you had to think about how these two avatars have been received in public or private spaces, are there any differences? And I would add one more thing to it. Are your avatars gay or not gay?

LENTCZNER: So Zarf is most definitely gay, because he's in-world married to Bam Bam, who is very decidedly male and who is in fact my real-life partner John. We are up front about that all around.

INTERVIEWER: It is not very common to see people chose an avatar of color if they themselves are white.

LENTCZNER: I see to some degree that Zarf is much more close to my slight distance from the norm. Obviously there's a fair bit of Middle Eastern Jew in my blood, when you look at me physically. And so, there's just a slight difference from the norm. And Zarf, I think, sort of hits that same distance, and that's because that's what feels comfortable to me.

INTERVIEWER: It's not a one-to-one difference that you represent. It's that he represents the same spread.

LENTCZNER: Right, exactly. And you know, it might have to do with a way that I can see to signify it. My Brooklyn accent isn't going to come through online.

INTERVIEWER: Well, a bit now.

LENTCZNER: Well, yeah, we have voice now. So it will.

INTERVIEWER: But with your Linden avatar, are you making a statement?

LENTCZNER: So that's a much more complicated thing. By the time I got around to choosing my Linden avatar, I had been in [the Second Life] world probably five months. I have to say, part of it is certainly a statement. I felt that in the world in general, I didn't see as much ethnographic diversity and specifically African-American representation as I thought there ought to be. So that's certainly part of it. Now, I might be slightly sensitized to that issue, due to my family's racial makeup [Mark and his partner John, who are both white, have two mixed-race children]. So that was certainly true. I also think choosing the kind of character had a lot to do with how I wanted to be perceived on first blush.

INTERVIEWER: Not as a white person?

LENTCZNER: No, you see, it was more about [how] I wanted to be slightly less...hip. What are the qualities I was looking for? Professorial. I wanted to be taken as someone who might have a story to tell or someone who might have something to say that might be worth listening to. I wanted to create a feeling of collegiality. So in fact, Zero almost often wears—it's horribly cliché—a tweed jacket. He has some other clothes, but he likes to make fun of the fact when he's wearing a t-shirt, because it just looks goofy on an older gentleman.

INTERVIEWER: Part of what you're telling me is the signifiers of age are equally as important as [those] of race and other identity markers. And you can't really separate them. If you were a young, buff, shaven-headed, hip black guy, that would be very different.

LENTCZNER: Completely. It's funny, no one's ever really said anything really racist to me in private or public spaces in Second Life. Oddly enough, people have said homophobic things to me.

INTERVIEWER: Oddly enough?

LENTCZNER: Well, it's not oddly enough. People made homophobic comments, but only after they recognized that I'm gay.

INTERVIEWER: Does race—or another of indication of difference like gayness—possess a kind of realness in a space where other things aren't?

LENTCZNER: Well, I'm guessing a little bit here, but I think it might have to do with the degree of distance, or the way in which you want people to think about you in relation to others. At least in twenty-first century Earth, I think race conveys a truth in a manner that being slightly shorter or not as well muscled doesn't.

INTERVIEWER: Can you explain to me what attracts you to virtual worlds?

LENTCZNER: I will try. But I will warn you, I am doing it with perfect 20/20 hindsight, and I'm doing it with having been in the industry. It's the ability to actually have a persona—even though I hate that term because persona implies artificiality. Actually what is important, [is] not whether the persona is me or is not me. It's the fact that it's complete enough to feel like a person. That's the important part.

3

Interview with the
Virtual Cannibal

An Appetite for the Virtual

You would think a virtual cannibal's biggest problem
would be that neither he nor his victims have bodies, but
you would be wrong. Gy is the avatar of a French white
male adult whose profession combines writer, translator,
and artist. In the summer of 2007, I met Gy through a
network of acquaintances in Paris. That spring had seen
the explosion of European Second Life (SL) participation,
particularly in France and Germany, and Gy emerged from
that European wave. He and I never met face to face, only
via our avatars. In that mediated form, Gy told me that in
this online experience *virtual cannibalism* had seized his
imagination. He participated in a gynophagia (eating woman) sex-play group that simulated sexual engagement that
includes rape, other forms of violent assault, asphyxiation,
and ultimately the death and consumption of the victim.
In short, he practiced virtual cannibalism as a sexual game.

To this end, the players use their avatars to role play as
dominant or submissive actors, engaging the verbal (text),
scripting (computer code), and graphical resources of the
platform to enact the scenarios. Part of the attraction for Gy

and other players who participate in this manner of sexual intercourse lay precisely in the transgression of the boundaries of postmodern culture. In terms of what may actually be done to another person (legally and morally), but also what may be represented as a desired activity, the virtual cannibals broke an inviolable taboo: eating human flesh.

Gy's story caught my attention first, because I became curious to understand what it might mean in a world without physical bodies to be a "cannibal." Recognizing that cannibalism is a crime outside of the virtual, it seemed additionally bizarre that virtual world participants would enact a ritual associated with the most primal of human urges, yet in a context of great abstraction—computer simulation. An implicit law of cyberspace had been to keep the "meat" out of information space; yet this group brought it right in, and with relish.

Second, in speaking with Gy, I found a charming and intelligent virtual world participant, with many opinions about what motivated him. Gy expressed an appetite for his virtual experience without shyness, embarrassment, or trepidation. His particularly self-aware tact—his knowingness and analysis of the situation—did not appear to diminish his pleasure in it. Additionally, Gy expressed this pleasure not as sexual pleasure (or not exclusively) but rather as titillation from the gestalt of virtual world engagement. From shared visualization to the code-based commands and typewritten conversation, he was excited not only by the content of the engagement (cannibalism), but its formal aspects as well. Thus, he presented an ideal mediated subject, neither enthralled by the technology he used nor immune to its attractions.

Life on the Screen

In *Life on the Screen*, a 1995 study of identity in the Internet age, Sherry Turkle writes of multiple identities as foundational to forming a sense of self. She notes, "The Internet is another element of the computer culture that has contributed to thinking about identity as multiplicity. On it, people are able to build a self by cycling through

many selves."[1] Her interviewees describe feeling "more like
myself" or "more like who I wish I was" in their Internet
identities. During the mid to late '90s, Turkle's concept of
cycling through identities became critical to a broader
understanding of network media adoption. In contrast,
I identify the media engagement of a contemporary networked generation as actual and persistent. Instead of
cycling through, we now work across and thereby extend
our sites of engagement. We have reached an end of the
virtual, as such, and entered an age of pervasive media.

In her work, Turkle describes the Internet as a space
away from everyday life, one that provides a laboratory to
test out ideas of self-image. Continuing her focus on multiplicity, she points out: "Now in postmodern times, multiple
identities are no longer so much at the margins of things...
The Internet has become a significant social laboratory for
experimenting with the construction and reconstruction of
self that characterize postmodern life. In its virtual reality,
we self-fashion and self-create."[2] Implicit in this analysis is
the bifurcation of the virtual and the real, allowing for a test
site outside of real-world consequences. I suggest that we
find today an enhanced connection between the virtual and
the physical world. If experimenting online defined much
of this first decade of social networked engagement, then
networked agency is the next turn.

It is in the vernacular of an everyday experience—the
extraordinary and the ordinary—that I argue for an understanding of networked media as augmentation of self and
world as opposed to fragmentation. This shift in perspective
is crucial for how we move forward in analysis, design, and
engagement of pervasive media. In the course of my field
research and analysis of media platforms, I have observed
that, as networked subjects, we exist in a realm of augmented reality, where our avatars (our online faces) represent us
in a persistent manner to a recognized community.[3] We can
date this shift to the turn of the twenty-first century, when
social media applications grew massively popular and became extensions of real life identities. At this point, media
users already regard pervasive networked engagement as a

1. Turkle, Sherry,
*Life on the Screen:
Identity in the Age of
the Internet* (New York:
Simon and Schuster,
1995), 140.

2. Ibid., 179–180.

3. From 2006-2008, I
did field research on
the subject of virtual
worlds, mobile media,
and X-reality design.
I interviewed (and
observed) media
designers, users, and
researchers in their
native contexts, which
included studio, confer-
ence, meetup, virtual
world, and laboratory.
See the introduction
to this book for a dis-
cussion of research
methods and scope.

4. The practice of identity consolidation does not preclude anonymous or alternate identities; in fact it is commonplace for users to have multiple log-ins. The reason for the multiple log-ins is the same as a decade ago: sometimes people want greater anonymity for their actions.

necessary supplement, or virtual prosthesis, built into the fabric of everyday life.

Within this context, persistence of identity as the dominant characteristic of network use represents one of the most profound cultural shifts of the Internet. This shift is played out in the growing hegemony of platforms, such as Facebook (a social network site with 500 million users as of 2010), that technically require one's profile to be authenticated. More importantly, Facebook demands a cultural authority, supported by its users, that platform participants properly identify themselves. Similarly, the success of professional networking sites such as LinkedIn are based on a contact network of true names and authorized links. In an increasingly spam-filled, criminal, and crowded Internet, one hears the call for authentication and identity management from users themselves. Projects such as OpenID and Higgins begin to address a growing interest in control of one's networked data.

Contemporary networked media use demonstrates less of an urge to cycle through identities as an interest to consolidate and protect identity.[4] The increasing anxiety around child safety on the Internet, the persistence of provocative and punitive behavior, and the sheer volume of information people face have moved the culture in a direction that might be described as increasingly filtered and insular. I would contrast Turkle's analysis of the Internet as a primarily experimental forum with a new form of network identity characterized by a strong sense of propriety around a virtual identity and the communities in which that self participates. The trend we see is that one's lived identity and one's life online move closer to each other as social network affiliations become more robust across media platforms and are paired with face-to-face gatherings.

Throughout the book, I have used the term X-reality to describe a shift from the binary engagement of virtual/real to a multi-vector engagement that spans types of connections. X-reality marks the variable spaces, places, and temporalities in which a network society exists, calling for an expanded vision of what comprises one's world. The question I ask Gy, and the analysis I provide of this community of media users, is what does it mean to create an actual experience using simulation as the primary tool?

Spectator of Your Life
In general, Gy describes his interest in Second Life as ancillary. He does not speak of the virtual world as critical to his sense of self or his relationships; he describes his participation essentially as casual. Gy ventured into the space sideways, by way of computer gaming and a philosophical interest in language. (In the virtual world, Gy quickly honed in on a pointedly erotic value of language, where the limitations of avatar communication advance a polarized discourse; language becomes more sexual and violent, as I discuss below.) Good graphics are important to him in video games, he explained, but it is primarily the chat as action, the language-based play in the virtual world platform that enticed him about Second Life.

Gy sums up his view of avatars with the observation that "you're the spectator of your life here," followed by the smiley face emoticon :) to underscore the nature of the text-based conversation we carried on during the course of the interview. In the recounting of his cannibal adventures, Gy enthusiastically exploits the rift between his presence in real life and the spectral presence of watching one's avatar do one's bidding. When he speaks of what he has done and seen through his avatar, Gy most often uses the third person "he," as opposed to saying "I." When I ask him about this split, the distance between him and the visible agent of his actions, he describes it as a symptom of simulation, a split between self and representation:

> Interviewer: "he" not "you" or "I"
> Gy: but then that works like in rl [real life] for
> that part well. [S]chizophrens from all countries
> get united!
> Interviewer: yah
> Gy: that could be the special SL sentence. lol.
> [Y]ou're the spectator of your life here. :)

5. Ken Hillis writes of the meaning of networked rituals in a time of pervasive media engagement, suggesting that the new territory we are encountering merges "transmission as a ritual and a ritual transmitted." Ken Hillis, *Online a Lot of the Time: Ritual, Fetish, Sign* (Durham: Duke University Press, 2009): 110–111.

6. Julian Dibbell, "A Rape in Cyberspace, or How an Evil Clown, a Haitian Trickster Spirit, Two wizards, and a Cast of Dozens Turned a Database into a Society," *The Village Voice*, (December 21, 1993): 36–42.

Gy's comment on the similarity of virtual and real life suggests that we encounter such rifts between self and self-perception every day, but that this schism is the very order of a mediated world.[5] And, at least for a period of time, Gy delighted in watching his life unfold in the acts of a "he" who stands in for "I."

As we proceeded in the interview, the subject expressed two basic sentiments about his virtual world engagement. He regularly referred to a sense of the unreality of life, disengagement, a feeling of ennui, and feeling outside of himself. And he regularly referred to the actuality of the simulated experience, describing the visceral responses on his part and other participants. In my analysis of our interview, I suggest that these are not contradictory sentiments. In his account, I understood not a bifurcation of real versus virtual, but rather a reflection and combination of the two states.

Out of the many interviews I conducted, I chose Gy's narrative as the subject of extended analysis because his experience highlights central issues of networked media, a culture of advanced simulation, and the role of an avatar as a subjective proxy. By exploiting the affordances of a virtual platform to its hyperbolic end—enacting the most extreme and violent of actions—the virtual cannibal becomes an instructive figure. He plays out in the extreme the options that a virtual world without consequences might offer, allowing us to consider whether, indeed, such a space exists. Are there acts, be they symbolic or simulated, for which there are no consequences? How do we comprehend simulation as it becomes increasingly visual and pervasive?

In 1993, two years before *Life on the Screen*, writer Julian Dibbell reported a rape in cyberspace. In a cover article for the *Village Voice*, Dibbell published a story that provided an important look at life online, particularly at the people who lived in multiuser, text-based virtual worlds.[6] His first-person report from the field of a MOO (a multi-user-dungeon-object-oriented world) described an online place of phantasmagoric beings experimenting in a magical world. The story Dibbell tells of Mr. Bungle, the extremist, the griefer, the troll is a story of one player bringing the specter of real violence (a rape) to an online world.

As with the players in Dibbell's tale of rape in cyberspace from the 1990s, because of its visceral nature the simulation of sexual violence forces a recalibration of the status of a virtual act. Gy and his loose cohort of virtual cannibals represent a complex engagement with the technical and cultural affordances of the platform they engage. I believe Gy is a figure who in his very extremity helps us to understand the limits of simulation and the expanding domain of the actual.

Rules of Engagement
I meet him first in Elpida, a picturesque virtual garden full of lush greenery and romantic walkways. Gy showed up as a small monkey that scampered about—his appearance the result of an avatar monkey suit that included animation scripting for motion. My avatar, Hapi, appeared in its bespoke Cute Robot form. Gy suggested we sit down to talk, a convention that has nothing to do with whether the avatar is tired or not, but rather with online gestures of human attention. As with the Lessig reading, sitting indicated that we were having a focused conversation. For the interview, we moved to a teahouse in Sokri, a Japanese-themed town (see figure 3.1). Over the course of our interview, Gy described an insular group that created a self-contained theatre of cruelty.

My first question for Gy was: what brought you to this particular platform, and what did you find when you arrived there? He explained that playing video games brought him to Second Life, but when he got there it was nothing like the first-person shooting game he had been used to playing. In fact, Gy said, "Second Life is boring as a video game." He expressed a feeling that many video game players feel in regard to social media platforms that do not have a specified action agenda: there is nothing to do, or rather there is only something to do if you invent it or find it. Gy pointed out that this kind of interaction made for some surprising discoveries. "The way you can interact with subjects is pretty

Interview with the virtual cannibal: Gy,
the virtual cannibal in his monkey-suit
avatar, and the author meet at the
Sokri teahouse in Second Life. Credit:
B. Coleman

Fig.3.1

amazing," he said. Unlike his prior experiences with video game avatars, Gy said, "the character you forge [in Second Life] starts to have his own history, just like in real life."

The refrain "just like in real life" winnows its way through the language of most virtual world players, regardless of genre or individual goals. In making the comparison between real and virtual, people grasp for a way to explain what it feels like to be somewhere perceptually, but physically not there at all. Gy uses the analogy to explain how Second Life presents a virtual experience that does not function as a game. But pause for a moment: if avatars running across a computer screen do not epitomize "gameness," then what does (see figure 3.2-3)?

Game designers Katie Salen and Eric Zimmerman define gaming as a "system in which players engage in an artificial conflict, defined by rules, that results in a quantifiable outcome."[7] The rule-based system with measurable result, as defined by Salen and Zimmerman, does not apply to largely social virtual world engagement. Yet much of what characterizes networked media design qualifies as game-like.

Specifically, it is a game of chance that facilitates Gy's movement across the virtual world. As one might speak of encountering a stranger in a foreign city, Gy speaks of luck or the chance encounter in the virtual domain.[8] His avatar accumulates a history, Gy says, "through the places he goes to, the persons he meets, and all that is based on chance." For example, he tells the story of his first meeting with the cannibal cult as a chance encounter.

"It really started," says Gy, "when I met a girl at the entry of one of these brothels and didn't enter it. She proposed me [sic] to play in a SL snuff movie. lol [laugh out loud]." He explained that in many ways a snuff film—making a movie where the actor is actually killed—is perfectly placed in a virtual context. "[T]hat's quite natural when you think about it," he reflected. "It is more death than life [in the virtual world], I guess."

In Western culture, sexual pleasure has been described as a petit mort—a little death. In his assessment of virtual representation—the mimetic space of simulation—Gy saw

7. Katie Salen and Eric Zimmerman, *Rules of Play* (Cambridge, MA: MIT Press, 2004), 96.

8. In the 1960s, sociologist Roger Caillois created a matrix of four basic categories of game play. Caillois, *Man, Play and Games*, trans. Barash (New York: Free Press of Glencoe, 1961). The categories are agon (contest), alea (chance), ilinx (vertigo), and mimicry (make-believe). Caillois also gave a gauge to read across the spectrum from the rule-governed (ludus) to the free-form (paidea). Social virtual worlds, as the point of greatest potential in mass media adoption and least known outside of niche, rest on the side of the game grid that hails the aleatory (chance) and the free-form (paidea). Those are the characteristics of social game play, but as we walk through several different kinds of social virtual worlds, we will encounter mixed degrees of alea and agon.

Virtual tourist: The author joins a hot
tub party in Second Life's Japan town,
where a Shogun Warrior also enjoys a
virtual soak. Credit: B. Coleman

Fig.3.2

Stumble upon: The author lands in the
middle of a satanic cabal on entering
the Second Life welcome area, October
2007. Credit: B. Coleman

Fig.3.3

9. Critical engagement
of BDSM includes
Thomas S. Weinberg,
*S & M: Studies in Dom-
inance & Submission,*
(Amherst: Prometheus
Books, 1995) and
Michel Foucault, "Sex-
ual Choice, Sexual Act,"
Foucault Live, (New
York: Semiotext(e),
1996): 322–334.

an imitation of death, not life. Thus, in his virtual play, Gy
made the "little death" literal. He took advantage of the
technical affordances and permissive culture he has found in
Second Life to launch an uncharted experience: to simulate
death. It is common for people to claim a life in a virtual
world that surpasses what they find in the real one. From
the paper and dice worlds of Dungeons and Dragons to
the graphically rich networked platforms, there is a long
history of participants claiming freedoms and happiness
in the virtual world that the real world could not provide.
Gy's testimony supports this claim, but with a distinct twist.
What he finds is not synthetic life but rather artificial
death as the way to augment his experience of the world.

Death, or rather killing, is represented in video games
thousands of times a second throughout the world, with war
and first-person-shooter games remaining the most popular
genre. In comparison to other forms of simulated violence,
virtual cannibalism is distinct in its systematic representation of rape and murder as a protracted, ceremonial act.[9]
With first-person-shooter games it is the act of shooting
that primarily absorbs the player. With virtual cannibalism
it is the sexualized staging of an execution. I observed in the
cannibals' activities a provocative intention to break societal
taboos. In their negotiation of simulation as an aspect of
networked media, I also saw qualities that are important for
understanding how to think about an increasingly mediated
world. Effectively, one finds in the cannibals' staging of death
both a critique of simulation and a dissolving of the boundaries between virtual and real.

Staging Death
In following the avatar he met in front of a virtual brothel,
Gy had essentially jumped down a rabbit hole in which
he would emerge as a participant in an online BDSM cult.
BDSM stands for bondage/discipline and sadism/masoch-
ism. The acronym covers an array of sexual practice that
includes domination and submission, punishment, role-
playing, and other activities, some with an erotic link to
cannibalism and snuff. The rigid protocol of BDSM role-

playing fits well within the context of a virtual world such as Second Life. In effect, the real-world role play creates a game structure for the open-ended design of the virtual platform. A discipline of identity and behavior can be imported into the virtual world. This engagement can, in fact, sustain the absence of real bodies and physical violence even while the symbolic register of the exchange remains intact.[10] Like other rule-based systems, this one—apart from what it signifies—establishes procedures for behavior to which participants abide.

In his description of this interplay, Gy speaks of a staging effect particular to his virtual-cannibal activities: removed from any particular attempt at realism, cannibals exploit the unreal aspects of simulation to amplify their actions. Using the visualization tools at hand, they create a spectacle for themselves and any other viewer online.[11]

Shouting to be Heard: Limits of Simulation
In entering the virtual world platform, Gy found a 3D rendering of places and avatars functioning in a real-time network. What the Second Life platform did not have, however, was specified rules of engagement. In the terms of service agreement, there were rules forbidding the destruction of virtual property and hate speech, but no guided play or specific procedural narrative as one might find in a computer game. In Second Life, participants were free to do what they liked. Or, to put it in different terms, in the absence of a specified engagement, participants filled the void with their own rules of engagement.

> Gy: [A]s I said many times in a 3D environment such as this one where you're completely free about what you wanna do, where sex seems to be one of the main attraction[s], you have to invent new ways of making it an experience. lol. And of course, it doesn't work at all. lol. Sex is the most boring thing here.

In the case of Second Life, the platform invites participants to create freely, and the instinct, as Gy narrates,

10. I use the term "symbolic" to mark a logic within a culture. As opposed to an imaginary state, the symbolic works as an aspect of how we understand the real. I draw my definition of the symbolic from the work of theorists such as Jacques Lacan, Claude Levi-Strauss, and Ferdinand de Saussure in the fields of psychoanalytic theory, structuralism, and semiotics.

11. Spectacle implies a visual demonstration. Implicit in the concept is the idea of exhibiting—something or someone is put on display. The literature on spectacle during different eras of technical reproduction, particularly the post-industrial period, is robust. For example, see Jonathan Crary, *Suspensions of Perception: Attention, Spectacle, and Modern Culture* (Cambridge, MA: MIT Press, 1999); Guy Debord, *The Society of the Spectacle*, trans. Donald Nicholson-Smith, (New York: Zone Books, 1999).

12. In their research
on online BDSM com-
munities, Shaowen
Bardzell and Jeffrey
Bardzell argue that
the graphical interface
of Second Life and an
aesthetics of BDSM are
mutually supportive.
Shaowen Bardzell and
Jeffrey Bardzell, "Docile
Avatars: Aesthetics,
Experience, and Sexual
Interaction in Second
Life," *People and
Computers XXI—HCI...
But Not as We Know
It: Proceedings of HCI
2007*, British Computer
Society 1 (2007): 3–12.

is to stage a sexual encounter.[12] He explained that often,
though not always, avatars initiated their entrance to the
platform by engaging another avatar in virtual sex. This
could be any combination of language (text-based chat),
visual animation (avatars in graphic engagement), or
computer-scripted behaviors applied to avatars, objects,
and environment.

In the interview, Gy describes virtual sex as both attractive—visually pulling one in—and boring as an act ("sex is
the most boring thing here"). What he implicitly points to
is the promise and limitation of simulation. I see this dual
condition of promise and limitation as a critical point in
how we understand networked media engagement and
how we frame the desire to use these platforms to connect
with each other. Perversely, or perhaps ingeniously, Gy saw
this limitation as an invitation to innovate.

What I observed in the virtual world engagement of
Gy and his cohort was that their verbal exchanges and
visual simulation pushed toward extreme forms. Instead
of a request, they would phrase something as a command.
They would represent bondage in lieu of sexual relations
of more equal terms. I understood this escalation in part
as a function of the mode of mediated communication.
Offline, Gy did not participate in extreme sex practices, yet
he rapidly escalated to a sadistic sexual engagement in this
virtual world. This behavior suggests not simply an issue
of agency—his subjective choice to be a participant—but
a structural aspect of the platform itself in which virtual
worlds provide an impetus for extreme behavior. Thus, we
see the drive toward the hyperbolic is built into the form
of mediation itself. One shares visualized space with
others, and yet the simulation lacks a perfect replication
of an embodied, unmediated encounter. As people try to
actually connect with each other, they grow excessive in
their communication.

Although the ability to participate in a networked 3D
space is a relatively new phenomenon, the technical limitations of life-like visualization and actions are apparent as
soon as one enters any of the existing platforms. Culturally,

we have limited practice with an open forum—a multiuser platform that is not a game but is in real-time. One ends up doing the mediated equivalent of shouting to get an actual response. One can see the human amplification of signal or gesture as part of the cycle of new media adoption.[13] Virtual worlds reach a threshold of simulation that cannot be crossed, even as what they appear to offer is exactly such a crossing.

In the interview, Gy addressed the radical behavior I observed, saying, "Considering you only have the chat to interact, most sexual relations are in BDSM." His remark points to an aspect of platform design that moves all exchanges to the level of bondage and discipline. With the cannibals, participants consciously escalate the terms of engagement, recognizing the limit of simulation and also exploiting it. Effectively, by graphically exclaiming, they seek a way to make the virtual more real. Their strategy does not address a technological solution—a better simulation as it were—but rather the translation of a set of procedures, BDSM's rules of engagement, to the virtual space.

Dolcett Girls

In sticking to the rules, a very rigid script of behavior, a group of players establishes a sense of the actual in the context of the virtual. Gy and the other participants keep their actions outside the realm of the real—no one was really killed and eaten—but within the emotional register of the real. Such a system of engagement can certainly exist offline. Marquis de Sade, a famously perverted eighteenth-century French noble, created a literary genre around what we now commonly call "sadism," in which behavior was carefully coordinated and staged so as to derive pleasure from inflicting pain or humiliation. De Sade wrote several books specializing in the sexual torture of young women, framing the works essentially as stylized manuals. In discussing how the protocol of sadism translates online, Gy cites de Sade to explain how the cannibals produce their staging, the *mise en scène*, or, in Gy's words, how they "make a picture through sexual intercourse." In this case

13. The first phone calls were shouted. The first films were composed of broad gestures and iconic tableaux. Early online communities such as the WELL and Nettime were punctuated with flame wars—the incendiary electronic missives sent by a few but observed by the entire group. Today, the customs for Internet teleconferencing and mobile telephony are developing in parallel with mass adoption of the technologies. One finds the same cycle with the new generation of virtual worlds.

the pictures are linguistic and visual. The procedural
elements—the manner in which the group utilizes the
technical possibilities of the platform—of the cannibal
experience include chat and scripted activities, which the
avatars graphically enact.

> Gy: [Y]ou go with someone in a special brothel
> and there is a room called Dolcett. [T]here, after
> the staging of a relation thru [through] chat you
> ask your partner to be cooked, selecting this script
> ball [virtual object with coded action inscribed]
> or that one. [A]nd then the partner can select an-
> other script ball to be the meal on the table. [T]he
> "master" selecting the one where he [will] "eat" an
> avatar. lol. I said to myself of course! cannibalism!
> as an evidence of [...*is typing*...] the cruelest thing
> when no more experience is possible.

Dolcett, the code for Gy's BDSM experience, originally
referred to the signature on a series of Internet-circulated
pornographic drawings that depicted submissive women
being hanged, cooked, and variously penetrated as part of
a sexual act. Dolcett or gynophagia role-play now extends
not only to that set of illustrations but also to an entire
subset of BDSM activity. The Dolcett scenario is often me-
dieval, borrowing from the fairytale structure of a young
peasant girl taken from her lowly position by the prince
to become the "queen for the day." Her rule ends in her
public execution, constructed for greatest erotic charge for
the crowd. Writer A. N. Roquelaure's (Anne Rice) popular
Sleeping Beauty soft-core BDSM series plays out for her
massive audience the basic stratagems of this role play. In
the case of Roquelaure's *Beauty*, it is a role reversal, where
the princess is forced to submit to machinations of a sexual
dominance order. One can find Dolcett fan fiction on the
Internet with titles such as "First Bite" and "How to Cook
Women's Breasts." There are also chat groups, web sites,
and, with the emergence of multiplayer virtual worlds,
avatar-based animation enacting Dolcett play.

The point I make in listing the various forums is that network culture in general has grown this illicit subculture into a forum essentially available to the cybertourist, by which I mean the casual web browser or visitor to a virtual world. It is not one platform or one circulating image, but a collection of searchable media that has taken root. In looking at online archives discussing this practice, I found that The Sims Online (TSO) appears to have hosted the first publicly manifest BDSM community. In comparison to the monumental and genre-changing successes of The Sims and Sim City, both single-player games, TSO, the first multiplayer offering in the series, did not succeed as a commercial hit. It was, however, successful with BDSM players.[14] With TSO, for the first time, one could essentially find 3D, fairly realistic depictions of humans that could be clothed (or naked), according to the player's interest. Additionally, the code scripts for these figures related to domestic human actions, such as intimate relations, as opposed to fighting moves as most video games do. With the leverage of a platform designed to simulate human relations, creative players adapted it to simulate the type of relations they chose.

This tradition carried over to Second Life, which emerged five years after TSO, as the next platform that allowed for human figures to be molded into any configuration imaginable. One virtual world blogger described her adventures in Second Life's Dolcett play much in the way one might outline learning to surf or another exotic experience explored on vacation:

> One of my more extreme fantasies involves Dolcett play. It's kinda weird. I don't like pain. Being whipped, paddled, or tortured really just turns me off. And the idea of snuff play just seems so... final. But the thought of being prepped, stuffed, basted, roasted and eaten...that appeals to me. I guess it goes back to my objectification fetish. Being turned into food is just as good as any other type of object. So, one of the many groups I joined

14. The Sims Online, Alphaville BDSM post, December 20, 2003, <http://www.bankhead. net/BlackRoseCastle/ Default.htm>.

15. "Roasted Yora,
$5.99 a pound,"
blogpost, February 11,
2007, <http://myslinsl.
blogspot.com/2007/
02/roasted-yora-
599-pound.html>.

16. Ibid.

[was] the Dolcett Girls group. A few days after
joining I got an IM [instant message] from [a
member].[15]

The blogger describes the act of being tied to a virtual spit
and having the apparatus narrate the progress of her being
cooked ("The machine was very interesting, giving a play
by play").[16] The blogger comments that she is surprised at
how much this experience arouses her. It is important to
note from the outset that, unlike a rape in cyberspace, the
online BDSM relations are consensual acts. Additionally,
as we are discussing their representation in a synthetic
computer-generated world, they are also simulated acts.
The blogger cited in the passage above, the interview with
Gy, and with other participants surveyed state that the
shared visual scenario of their avatars committing these
acts creates a powerful sense of an actual shared experience. Participants describe a twin sensation of observing
oneself and being the primary actor. Via mediation, they
had the sensation of being in two places at once. This
experience was not circumscribed by a technically perfect
simulation but, rather, the various levels of human expression the players embedded in the platform.

I am suggesting that the promise and limitation of simulation needs to be understood not only in terms of design
(including technical affordance) but also in the terms of
people's engagement of a medium. The marker of mediation
did not fall away (e.g., the virtual spit narrates the act of
cooking); yet participants found ways to satisfy their interests. In their work on remediation, new media theorists
Jay Bolter and Richard Grusin talk about the "logic of
transparent immediacy" that is designed into new media
forms. They argue that media are designed to disappear
and leave the user with a sense of immediacy in mediation.
However, I would suggest that, in fact, we find the opposite
effect when considering users' experience of networked
media: a medium does not need to disappear for users
to still feel profoundly connected to mediated acts. The
particular group discussed in this chapter is pointedly

self-aware of the nature of a medium and the act of mediation. Despite the fact that the frame of mediation remains,
they understand that their acts make an impression; these
acts effect change in the participants. In other words, the
participants do not see the BDSM role play as a game in
a game world but as the rituals of their cult. In this sense,
they see their virtual behavior as actual.

Virtual Solitaire

"I'm not even really here," hip-hop artist El-P snarls on
Fantastic Damage (Definitive Jux, 2009), an album-long
trip through contemporary landscapes barren and forlorn.
His sentiment of alienation and isolation are symptomatic
of many people. Several studies inform us that Americans
in particular are lonelier than ever, lacking human contact
and the confidences of close friendship. Political scientist
Robert Putnam's work on social networks, particularly the
book *Bowling Alone*, makes central in academia and mass
media the discussion of a changing social system. Also
on that subject, the paper authored by sociologists Miller
McPherson, Lynn Smith-Lovin, and Matthew E. Brashears,
"Social Isolation in America: Changes in Core Discussion
Networks over Two Decades," sends an alarming message
on the decline in civic engagement in the United States.
They conclude that we have grown more insular and less
engaged with other people and contexts.[17]

Yet, during the same period and with the same population, research groups such as Pew Research Center,
MacArthur Foundation, and the Annenberg Center for the
Digital Future report that more people use the Internet
than ever before and that their "relationships developed
via mediated communication are as valuable to them
as their real world friends and family."[18] *The Strength
of Internet Ties*, a 2006 study by the Pew Internet and
American Life Project for the Pew Research Center, characterizes a strong sense of activism in Internet use: not
only are people finding affinity groups over the Internet
but those networks often cross over into relationships that
exist in the world, face-to-face.[19]

17. Miller McPherson,
Lynn Smith-Lovin, and
Matthew E. Brashears,
"Social Isolation in
America: Changes in
Core Discussion Net-
works over Two De-
cades," *American
Sociological Review* 71
(June 2006): 353–375.

18. 2007 *Digital Future
Report*, Center for the
Digital Future, USC
Annenberg School,
www.digitalcenter.
org; Joseph Kahne,
Nam-Jin Lee, and Jes-
sica Timpany Feezell,
"The Civic and Political
Significance of Online
Participatory Cultures
among Youth Transi-
tioning to Adulthood,"
DML central Working
Papers, MacArthur
Network on Youth &
Participatory Politics,
Digital Media and
Learning initiative (Feb-
ruary 2011), <http://
www.dmlcentral.net>.

19. J. Boase et al., *The
Strength of Internet
Ties*, Pew Internet &
American Life Project,
Pew Research Center,
January 25, 2006,
<http://www.
pewinternet.org>.

20. Raph Koster, round table with Howard Rheingold and Cory Ondrejka. Metaverse U, Stanford University, Stanford California, 2008.

The Pew Internet study concludes that people find their online relationships as valuable as their real-world friends and family because much of the virtual exchange develops into actual friendship that exists online and off. Additionally, the exclusively virtual friendships offer powerful connections unto themselves, although the condition of friendship is not based on face-to-face encounters. As game designer Raph Koster quipped at a conference on virtual worlds, all actual relationships become synchronous at some point.[20] Be it over the phone or via VoIP, meeting in real-time fulfills a crucial part of relationships, even if it is not face-to-face.

These research reports support my finding that increasingly we experience a sense of the actual in our mediated exchanges. However, the qualities and consequences of these exchanges—what I have termed networked agency—is largely dependent on how we situate that engagement. The virtual cannibal used his reach to enact violence and, as I have argued, there is a tendency to "shout" or amplify one's message in a hyperbolic way when engaging new media platforms. The mandate of pervasive media engagement, in this case, is twofold. First, we must recognize that people are addressing each other. Second, we must also move toward a media culture in which participants recognize a shared subjectivity as opposed to a mutual objectification.

The reports on the unprecedented loneliness of Americans, such as "Social Isolation in America," and the Pew Internet report on the richness of network ties present two different results that seemingly go in opposite directions. I would suggest that the reports speak to the same issue from different perspectives. "Social Isolation in America" tells us that the social animal that we are has run smack into the uprooted creatures we have become, as we see with the new millennium's accelerated fragmentation of family, neighborhood, and nation. The Pew Internet study tells us that affinity groups are thriving, but the connections are configured along new lines that often defy the demarcation of territory or blood. We find the dissolution of traditional frames of community and society, even as we relocate ourselves across networks of affiliation. The critical

aspect to grasp is the value of networked engagement in
moving toward a better understanding of agency in the
twenty-first century.

21. Kevin Driscoll, personal interview, May 15, 2009.

Designed for Exposure
In the mid 1990s, when graphic information, particularly
still images in jpeg format, became ubiquitous, a web community called E/N (everything/nothing) created an exercise
in radical boredom by posting text and, often, images in
which users would vie to outdo each other in debasement.
One series focused on body amputations. The first poster
in the chain cut off the tip of his finger and uploaded the
before-and-after shots for proof. The next player in the
series cut his finger off to the first knuckle and offered those
images as one-upmanship...and so on until the chain could
no longer be sustained or people lost interest.

While the demonstration of daring for an audience of
peers exists in every subculture, this bodily abasement
of a late-night network exchange contains a particular
tone of self-loathing combined with mean spiritedness
that only seems to have increased with the expansion of
network culture. A massively popular website in the 2010s
for all things E/N, the 4chan /b/ board, marked as "random"
entries, held a contest one night, initiated by a user, where
boys posted photos trying to outdo each other in a "who
has the smallest penis" contest.[21] Thankfully, players did
not bring amputation to bear in this competition.

From a decade ago to the early twenty-first century,
behind the screen of online anonymity we see that people
continue to express deep feelings to virtual strangers. More
often now we have faces attached to these actions and trace-
able identities attached to these faces. People treat networked
forums less like masked balls or other forms of role play
and more like experiences they claim for themselves.

Certainly people use false identities and other forms of
masking to make their acts anonymous. In the case of the
virtual cannibal, I would say Gy uses virtuality as a forum
for exposure, much like the spectacle of E/N and 4chan /b/.
Even if he chose a particularly horrible mode of expression,

he uses networked media in much the same way as the millions of people posting homemade video to YouTube: they are creating images of themselves and their acts that they design for exposure, for the greatest degree of circulation and spectatorship—their own and others'. What we find with Gy, and what we often find in the current state of networked media, is a graphic urge, an urge to show, characterized by a mediated form of shouting. Participants often chose provocative language and images to make an impression, to connect.

I interviewed a man, a father of a teenage girl, who expressed dismay when he found that his child had taken pictures of a neighbor in the shower and then posted the images to her profile page on Facebook. In terms of the media sphere, several things have changed to enable the girl's behavior. She has a digital camera from which images can instantly and easily be uploaded to a website. Additionally, she and her social group engage with a web-based profile page every day, making it an important communication forum for them. The teen possesses the means (camera with easy web upload) and the motivation (valued peer network space) to actualize the desire to impress her peers. In this case, the problem is not the tools, but rather how the girl used them.

Thus, the father's unhappiness with his daughter arose not from her access to media but from her lack of judgment. He understood that his daughter could take illicit photos, but he could not fathom why she would post them to an essentially public forum. Teen pranks have never gone out of style. I would suggest that peeking at the naked neighbor falls within that category, but giving friends (and strangers) searchable media broadens the scale, and thus the impact, of the act. Searchable media means that if the creator labels the photo "naked old guy" and I query my search engine for images of "naked old guy," then I may very well find the picture of the teenager's neighbor in the shower. Do I know him? No. But somebody does. Posting images or any other media online creates an archive of the image outside of the photographer's control. Networked media creates a new precedent for the autonomy of a piece of media once it begins to circulate.[22] The image can be copied and circulated infinitely. In this sense, an act that may have been temporary, even though transgressive (such as spying on someone), becomes in its media form essentially indelible. In extending our reach with networked media, we find new conditions of actual consequences.

If bullying remains a largely local phenomenon, the aspect of online harassment among peers, otherwise known as cyberbullying, engages the affordances of pervasive media. This is a growing phenomenon that underscores the increasingly central place of networked media in everyday life. Defamatory images, gossip, and direct messages of ill intent circulate with great speed to the target and among the peer group. In this sense, bullying is no longer localized at school or at the park, but is omnipresent.

For the teenager, she and her friends live more publicly than any generation before them. We see new strategies around self-presentation in which networked subjects negotiate what to show in a culture in which there is a demand to do so.[23] With the perception of living in the public eye, we see with network culture, and particularly with youth, what looks like a rise in exhibitionism—exposing oneself as well as others. The teen girls might have taken the nude pictures of her neighbor spontaneously. In posting them online, she made a considered act. It may not have been an act of cyberbullying, per se, as the victim was neither targeted nor part of the girl's social group. Nonetheless, in holding him up for ridicule her primary goal was to demonstrate prowess in mediated form to her peers.

The heat of the moment does not account for the kinds of games played on the early Web of E/N sites, more recently on the 4chan /b/ board, or practices of cyberbullying. Though dark in their tenor, these exchanges are pointed examples of the urge to show closely coupled with a desire to connect across media channels. We are newly armed with the technical additions of visualization and increasingly shared time or spatial media connections. One already sees the agency of networked subjects in the ability to affect one's context and community—even if the effect is a negative one.

22. "Burt is Evil" represents one of the most famous examples of this in Internet lore. Artist Dino Ignacio created the Internet meme taking the beloved Muppet character Burt (of Sesame Street fame) and circulating images of the yellow moppet wearing an evil scowl. Eventually, the "Burt is Evil" image appeared on an Osama bin Laden rally poster in Afghanistan as an anti-American icon ripped directly from the web. On the personal level for Ignacio the global flow of his image made his life more difficult. But on the network level, this was an uncannily precise demonstration that you never know where something you launch will end up. Dino Ignacio, personal interview, ROFLcon conference on Internet memes, MIT, Cambridge MA, 2008.

23. Social media scholars Helen Nissenbaum and danah boyd have made the point in their work that despite the fact that networked media can carry images and information faster and farther than before, people, including teenagers maintain a strong sense of privacy. They both ask that the context must be taken into consideration the nature of what looks like self-exposure. See Helen Nissenbaum, "Privacy As Contextual Integrity," *Washington Law Review*, vol. 79, 2004: 101-139; danah boyd "Living Life in Public: Why American Teens Choose Pubicity Over Privacy," paper, Association of Internet

Researchers, Gothen-
burg, Sweden, 2010,
<http://www.danah.
org/papers/talks/2010/
AOIR2010.html>.

As pervasive media grows as a global condition, one is faced
with increasingly pressing issues of media use and its design.
With given channels of communication do we behave in
a preordained manner? Can we use networked media to
support social norms that are libratory as opposed to a
recapitulation of the punitive? Does the rise of networked
subjects necessitate societal change?

Change of Virtual Heart
Toward the end of the interview, Gy stated that the real key
to creativity with networked media lay in designing tools.
To his mind, the most powerful thing one could do was
control an environment, not just the actors within it. After
exhausting the cannibal play, he found his new creative
outlet in designing virtual furniture.

> Interviewer: What about furniture? not as inter-
> esting ;-)
> Gy: Yes it is! It's just like getting involved in the
> technical secrets of sl [Second Life]. Much more
> serious and interesting than sex here. There is
> a hard selection on that basis. Everybody CANT
> script or make buildings or whatever. I tried
> scripting. It's a hell.

Ironically, it is only in discussing technical secrets of the
platform that Gy remarks that a virtual experience is "hell,"
despite the fact that he had spent the course of the interview
recounting stories of simulated hell for others.

And with that change of orientation, a quixotic shift of
temperament, Gy bid adieu to his first virtual adventure,
and turned toward a culture that he felt represented real
secrets and power: building simulations. He and the other
participants had succeeded in wrapping real-world experience around a virtual common ground. They had reached
each other, for better or for worse, and after that point
there was only repetition of a scripted engagement.

Gy did not get his just desserts from cooking women.
He did not suffer public humiliation among his peers for

playing vicious games. He was not ejected by game wizards from the world he inhabited. He moved on to the next thing that caught his attention. No punishment emerged for his time as a virtual cannibal perpetrating unspeakable acts. But neither does the absence of public sanction mean that these acts did not occur. One can comprehend his shift from virtual cannibal to would-be virtual architect as a continuum, as opposed to a break.

Gy had reoriented content, yet his focus on making the virtual manifest as objective experience persisted. By enacting the logic of code, he would once again see his ideas manifest as objects and actions for all to witness. This time it would be toward the construction of the environment as opposed to the spectacular. In terms of his overall behavior, one sees Gy's engagement in the virtual world driven by a desire for mastery. Whether uttered to an avatar or written as a line of code, he demonstrated to himself that a command could in fact be an act.

In his virtual cannibal engagement, Gy brought to his participation a sense of exhaustion, not personal but societal. He expressed the feeling that we have reached a limit of human experience, which led him to seek the unsavory in order to provoke a sensation in himself and others. This kind of thrill-seeking has a long tradition that tracks back to eighteenth-century libertines, nineteenth-century opium eaters, and cultural transgressives of all centuries. The new turn Gy expresses reflects a jump in scale of ennui and alienation. A generation of networked subjects seems to suffer from it. We find ourselves constructing terrible games in order to amuse ourselves, games that have no borders.

The test sites of the 1990s online world described by Turkle marked a space away from our real lives. In looking at the extreme practices of various networked groups, one can say that virtual cannibals did not invent sexual perversion; they simply made it easier to find. For various reasons, these types of subcultures once lurked in the shadows, on the periphery of a city and society. Now we find them in the broad daylight of any search engine. Does that change the nature of the subculture, or does it change the sensibility of those of us who had previously been shielded from it because it was more difficult to access?

Gy had no previous experience with this culture and its explicit markers before entering the virtual world. Looking for a new experience, he found one. The virtual cannibals finding Gy, and Gy finding them, represents a combination of coincidence, thrill-seeking, and predisposition of platform; he made himself available to the experience. In one sense, the cannibals exploit virtual space in exactly the same way that other explorers and innovators have since its inception: they create space apart, a space not subject to rules of gravity any more than the rules of society. For testing boundaries and trying out new roles, the location could not be better. Role-playing in the safe space of games over the Internet represents a long tradition. It all works very tidily: real experience resulting in no real harm done and lots of stories for the friends.

Yet, alas, the answer is no. No, the story does not end with a virtual thrill ride; no, because we already ask more of and give more to the worlds we make. Perhaps most importantly, the virtual does not remain safely in its own domain because the exchange between simulated and lived is not unilateral. The channels of communication open in both directions. As a society, we are beginning to recognize the importance of pervasive media not only in how it connects us to other people, but also in how it reflects patterns of perception and behavior of self and world. Even among casual users of virtual platforms, we do not find a safety net of a world entirely apart. The walled gardens of past role-playing games, if they ever truly existed, are now porous.

Not everyone will become a virtual cannibal. The virtual platform Gy used advertised itself as a fantasy life made graphic, which in the case of the cannibals became a technological seduction they could not resist. The cautionary tale we learn from Gy's story provides greater insights on the culture of networked media use and design than as a parable against virtual cannibalism. We learn that the more we rely on a fantasy of a second self—a self outside of the persistence of identity and continuous relationships—the more we risk the casual violence that states of alienation induce (see figure 3.4).

Throughout, I have spoken of networked media as an augmentation to everyday life, not as a source itself of violence or any other type of expression. As actors in this network, if there is to be agency, we must ourselves locate responsiveness and responsibility. It would be a mistake, though, to understand this position as a fully autonomous agency, a sovereignty as such. In analyzing how a medium behaves—how it is designed and what people do with it— we also acknowledge that the networked subject participates within the network. We are not outside of the augmented reality we engage, even if we are not enslaved by it. In his media practice, while Gy recognizes the limits of simulation as a technical forum, he does not see the power of networked agency as a necessarily contingent one: a position outside of mastery in its traditional terms. He is not alone in his conflation of signals, mixing new media practices with old forms of relation.

If we compare the network experience in the early twentieth-century to that of a decade ago, we see that we have an increased number of media channels by which we recognize each other. Additionally, we find increasingly porous paths between online and offline identities. Instead of discrete incidents of virtual play or real-life work, what we find growing in scale are experiences of networked subjects who engage multiple spaces of agency.

Network Society
In *The Rise of the Network Society*, sociologist Manuel Castells argues that identity formation in the information age stands outside the historical processes we have known. He sees a global network effect in which groups of individuals organize and validate their perspective as a community. Castells calls this a societal shift, where we have moved away from traditional forms of authority and toward a powerful manifestation of communal affirmation of identity. I see in pervasive media engagement a sign of the network society Castells describes, where we situate ourselves as subjects in a changing landscape.

Get a first life: A widely circulated
image from a satire site, GetaFirstLife.
com, posted by writer Darren Barefoot,
reminding people to get a real life and
not only a virtual one (2007). Credit:
Darren Barefoot

Fig.3.4

In the postmodern fragmentation of inherited social structures such as family, neighborhood, and nation, Castells sees the potential for the active engagement of "resistance cultures," identities formulated across geographic boundaries. His theory offers a model of community as that which forms itself in resistance to the normative culture, gaining the power of self-definition and even the ability to change the very structure of society. In addition to discussing the rise of a networked computing culture, Castells gives examples of the emergence of global factions of fundamentalism and an international women's movement—notably, groups that may use technology but are not defined by a mediated communications system. His larger point is that a global network changes the experience of the world for all, not only for those with accelerated technology use.

23. Manuel Castells, *The Power of Identity: The Information Age: Economy, Society and Culture*, vol. 2 (Malden, MA: Wiley-Blackwell, 2004), 7.

Castells sees a communal affirmation of identity as emblematic of a network society. On this subject he writes, "I propose the idea that in the network society for most social actors, meaning is organized around a primary identity (that is an identity that frames the others), which is self-sustaining across time and space."[23] In this concept of a persistent identity within a network society, we find a majority culture breaking into smaller affinity groups that behave like communal groups, where faith or ethnic heritage carry more weight than citizenship. If we follow Castells's logic, we end up in a place that is both a return to another earlier time in social organization and also an unprecedented time in the global outlook of network connections.

In the early years of the twenty-first century, the arguments rage around how much agency we have as individuals, how media technologies affect our sense of agency, and what degree of agency we ascribe to the machines themselves. We hear this discussion among scientific researchers and media theorists as well as between parents and their children. Castells' analysis forecasts an enormous change in how we understand ourselves as social actors in light of becoming networked subjects. In networked communities, people increasingly define themselves in terms of their tribe—their affiliation group—that is not based on geographic location or physical state. What we see are people forming affiliations contingent on their networks: even if I have a plethora of avatars, I only have one identity. I form that identity based on the strength of my network; it reflects the "me" I think I am. The power of identity in a network culture, as Castells tells us, rests in the power of self-transformation. In this case, the network society recognizes a newly extended gravitas to the virtual. Its actuality has become a vivid aspect of lived experience. As opposed to presenting a world apart, pervasive media use facilitates an augmentation of the world in which we live.

In ancient Rome, *persona* indicated one's public face as a citizen; persona represented moral standing and civic image. For a period of time in the early 1990s, a small group of computer game designers referred to what is now commonly called an "avatar" as a "persona." At this point in time and on a much larger scale, one finds the ancient use of persona renewed with a twenty-first century meaning, where virtual persona bears cultural weight. The increasing value of the virtual relates to a larger understanding of network society. Just as email became a valid form of mediated communication two decades ago, in the trajectory of network culture we see increasingly broad bands of virtuality included in daily life. We can still differentiate between mom and her dragon avatar, but when her avatar waves to us from one networked platform or another, we wave back. We already recognize her actual gesture conveyed via mediation, just as we can interpret what it means when somebody blows us a kiss.

Virtual Cannibal Transcript (Excerpt)
What follows is an interview with Gy, the avatar of a French white male adult whose profession combines writer, translator, and artist. Gy ventured into the virtual world Second Life by way of video gaming and a philosophical interest in language. Once there, he joined a virtual cannibal cult. In the chapter "Interview with the Virtual Cannibal," I discuss Gy's exploits in the virtual world. Here, in an excerpt from the transcript, the reader can see the tempo and tone of the interaction. I have included the timestamps as they appeared in the original context of the virtual world dialogue.

Location: a teahouse in Sokri, on the Second Life (SL) platform, May 19, 2007

[6:27] INTERVIEWER: what brought you into SL and what did you find when
        you arrived?
[6:27] GY: video games, that's what brought me to SL
[6:27] GY: I used to hate chats
[6:27] INTERVIEWER: yeah, but this is boring as a video game
[6:27] GY: you mean ...
[6:27] GY: SL?
[6:27] GY: yeah
[6:28] GY: it's often boring
[6:28] GY: but the way you can interact with subjects is pretty amazing
[6:28] INTERVIEWER: video games narrate an experience with much more
        tempo. i agree, it is the interaction that sets this apart.
[6:28] GY: completely
[6:29] GY: to me, it's not a game in that sense there's nothing to play with
[6:30] GY: the character you forge starts to have his own history
[6:30] GY: just like in RL [real life]
[6:30] GY: through the places he goes to
[6:30] GY: the persons he meets
[6:30] GY: and all that is based on chance
[6:30] INTERVIEWER: 'he; not 'you' or 'i'
[6:30] GY: but then
[6:30] GY: that works like in rl for that part
[6:31] GY: well
[6:31] GY: schizophrens from all countries get united!
[6:31] INTERVIEWER: yah
[6:31] GY: that could be the special SL sentence
[6:31] GY: lol
[6:31] GY: you're the spectator of your life here
[6:31] GY: :)

John Swords: From Bulletin Boards to the Metaverse

Over the past two decades, John Swords has transformed himself from network hobbyist to media professional, creating a web company and later joining Electric Sheep Company, a design group for online worlds. Swords went on the Internet in the early 1990s, joining a local bulletin board service (BBS). He discovered with the BBS format—modem dialup and local connections—a rich online community. From BBS to an emergent metaverse (a pervasive media world), Swords continues to keep the quest for community at the core of his experiences.

Location: Metaverse U Summit, Stanford University, February 17, 2008

SWORDS: It was 2003 or so. And what I found when I went into Second Life was that there really wasn't a whole lot for me to do there other than to socialize, because I wasn't a content creator. I realized that probably my skills would best be used for business. I bought a bunch of currency, probably a few thousand dollars worth of currency. I found three guys who were dressed like Italian mafia in-world and immediately I realized that there was not a good reputation system and I had no link to their real-life identity or any type of identity.

INTERVIEWER: What other systems do have it? With the bulletin boards reputation was implicit because it was a known community. You didn't actually have markers. Next to my name, you don't see a +10 for reputation. It's just implicit.

SWORDS: Well the IRC [Internet relay chat] channels that I used to hang out in and bulletin boards, we had something that Second Life doesn't have, and that is a concept of local. And so I would hang out two or three times a month with people. And so that was a way to translate the reputation.

INTERVIEWER: But with IRC, participants didn't have to be geographically bound.

SWORDS: They didn't have to be, but those are the ones that I usually hung out with. There's a story that's documented in the *BBS The Documentary* about how a woman ran a board, she had an affair with one of her users. She was married. That night at three a.m. all the people on the board were called and they went to her rescue because the husband found out. They all went physically to her house, helped her pack her stuff and get her out. You don't hear about stories like that very often online today because there is no local element like you had back then. Yeah. That local element really solved that identity issue.

INTERVIEWER: So when do I get that violin song on meeting each other in virtual space being so much more meaningful? But what is it that attracts you to continuing to work and play in something like a virtual world?

SWORDS: Well, because I think that all those issues of reputation and ownership are solvable issues. Facebook is a Web-based social network that basically has come up with game mechanics around human relationships.

INTERVIEWER: [Facebook] is easy to get, the structure is clear, so it's making a game out of friendship.

SWORDS: That's what Facebook does. I think that what needs to happen is a mapping of social interactions into game mechanics within a virtual world. There's so much work to be done there about just connecting people. With Second Cast [the virtual world podcasts Swords initiated] I felt...there wasn't enough media and coverage of things going on in virtual worlds. Podcasting was fairly new. And it's a great indie platform for getting content distributed. So I wanted to talk to people about what was going on in the virtual world. I initially put out a note on the forums and said, I'm looking for people [who] have been here for a while who understand what's going on. And I want to do a weekly radio show format that will be distributed so people [who] are not in virtual worlds can tune in too. Reznation.com is where all of my audio stuff is. I put a note out on the forums, and then I got some emails from some people. Mark Wallace responded to me.

INTERVIEWER: This was before he was involved with the *Second Life Herald* [an online newspaper about the virtual world]?

SWORDS: This is when he was with the *Herald*. Lordfly Digerido, who is Josh Eikenberry, he was one of the first builders in Second Life [who] responded. Also Cristiano, who was a scripter programmer. Torrid was a content creator. And then it was the journalist, Mark [Wallace], who basically rounded up the group. It was a roundtable of five of us. We hadn't met each other when we started. If there's one thing to take away from Second Cast, it was that here was a group of five people, that when you listen to us, it sounds like you're talking to a group of really good friends and clearly we had never met. We had no real-life ties to one another.

Presence

Desert of the Real

In describing the problem of simulation, the Argentinean writer Jorge Luis Borges wrote a twentieth-century parable about a guild of cartographers who created a map the actual size of an empire. "On Exactitude in Science," the title of the piece, describes a map "which coincided point for point with [the empire]."[1] In the hubris of the scientists—their passion for rigor of measurement and modeling—they fail to see the meaninglessness of the act: in rendering the world as simulacrum, an image of itself, they obscured rather than illuminated the knowledge of the world as such.

As the story reveals, subsequent generations abandon the map to the Deserts of the West, where it becomes the tattered shelter for wild animals and vagabonds. In this chapter on virtual presence, I ask what kind of measure scientists in experimental psychology, computer science, and sociology bring to bear on our understanding of a networked subject. The research projects I analyze below address how we experience a culture of pervasive media and increasingly robust simulations of presence.

1. Jorge Luis Borges, "On Exactitude in Science," *Jorge Luis Borges, Collected Fictions*, tran. Andrew Hurley (New York, NY: Penguin, 1999).

2. Jean Baudrillard,
Selected Writings, ed.
Mark Poster (Stanford,
CA: Stanford University
Press, 1998), 166–184.

The problem of simulation is an old one and precedes computational and digital culture. In essence, simulation poses the problem that we may mistake the virtual for the real. For our concerns regarding avatars and a generational shift to pervasive media engagement, the nature of both technological design of and cultural practices with simulation has also changed. We are not so much in danger of mistaking the simulacrum for the thing itself. Rather, we are in a time when simulating presence has become a standard aspect of how we understand a full engagement with one another. Today the most intimate of relationships often includes mediation. Instead of mediated communication functioning as a simulacra—a stand in for the face-to-face encounter—as a society we have begun to use networked media to maintain a pervasive presence with each other. What is at stake is the framing of the face-to-face experience as the exclusive site of the authentic and the real. And, in tandem, we also reassess the situation of agency within a distributed network.

The most important characteristics of networked media and networked subjectivity align in the phenomenon of virtual presence (the sense of being somewhere via mediation) and, the closely related term, copresence (the sense of being together with others via mediation). With the emergence of pervasive media, the questions I ask in terms of the value of simulation are: how are presence and copresence designed as aspects of networked media technologies? And, critically, how do we perceive and engage presence as an aspect of simulation?

Avatar Presence

My argument counters that of philosopher Jean Baudrillard in his famous treatise on the seduction of simulacra, *Simulacra and Simulations*. As I discuss in chapter 1, Baudrillard writes about the clouded vision of our time, and he uses Borges' confederacy of mapmakers as the figure of a blinded postmodern culture.[2] The hyperreal is the word Baudrillard uses to describe a world already adrift in a sea of simulation long in advance of a popular use of the Internet.

In his view, Disneyland and other closed gardens of entertainment keep us distracted from the poverty of the real: alienation, objectification, fragmentation, loss, and bondage all characterize what is left of the postmodern subject enthralled by a virtual world. A key point that Baudrillard makes is that there is no outside to this experience of simulation. We are enveloped in a technological sublime and left abject in a total disorientation. To the contrary, I am suggesting that in the forty-some years during which we have moved to a digital society and networked world we see aspects of simulation engaged toward agency and mutual presence, i.e., we have moved toward an actual.

In effect, the primary purpose of using an avatar is to conjure presence. They mark our sense of being there together when we are physically apart. And, in this sense, avatars are a product of computational simulation that gesture toward a state of the actual—an effect across sites of engagement. At this moment in pervasive media, we can locate an engagement of simulation that works toward an experience of agency as opposed to a de facto state of abjection.

The key difference between a historical assessment of simulation as deception (such as Baudrillard, Guy Debord, and others have argued) and simulation as an aspect of copresence—being together via mediation—is the dialogic aspect of networked media technologies.[3] Historically, in arguments such as Debord's Society of the Spectacle, one finds a powerful argument for mass media spectacle as a simulation of the real in the service of enthralling the public.[4] Unlike film, television, or even Disneyland, i.e., classic "technologies" of mass media spectacle, we find with networked media—in technical affordance and cultural practice—the capacity for feedback as a form of situated agency. (As I discussed in chapter 1, situated agency describes one's perception that one can affect change in the world.)

I am not suggesting that with pervasive media (in contrast to mass media or even early Internet culture) we have found a panacea against mediation as obfuscation. I am arguing though for a recognition of increased capacities of copresence. I address here what I see as practices around

3. The terms dialogic refers to the concept established by literary theorist Mikhail Bakhtin to describe literary texts in conversation with other works. In Bakhtin's view, most forms of expression are dialogic, i.e., they are in continual dialogue with both past and future expressions. To call a text or a media platform—in my rendition—a dialogic form, it is to recognize how it may be informed or changed by people's engagement of it.

4. Guy Debord, *Society of the Spectacle*, trans. Donald Nicholson-Smith (New York: Zone Books, 1994), 67.

5. In comparison, I would point to a paper such as "SIMULA-TION 101: Simulation versus Representation," ludologist Gonzalo Frasca's 2001 reassessment of simulation in society. In my view, Frasca makes an essentially technologically deter-minist argument in his discussion of simula-tion as exclusively the ability to create 3D models of the world. He removes simula-tion from its broader societal implications by making it primarily an issue of computer-generated representa-tion. Gonzalo Frasca, "SIMULATION 101: Simulation versus Rep-resentation," (2001), <http://www.ludology. org/articles/sim1/simu-lation101.html>.

media engagement and not exclusively technological development.[5] In looking at media practices, I would suggest that the issues of ethics, perception, and objectifi-cation are not ameliorated by a technical analysis of simu-lation. Rather, I see interrelated aspects of practice, design, and perception to be critical to a holistic understanding of what we do with media simulation and how, as a society, we comprehend it. In this sense, I understand avatars as emblematic figures of contemporary copresence.

As I discuss below in reference to experimental work with avatars, one of the effects of avatar mediation is that we externalize and objectify our utterances, expressions, and gestures. As an avatar may have a face, so too, our emails, IMs, and SMS create an archive of our expressions and days. Two important issues emerge as a consequence of continual externalization of expression. First, in the phenomenon of avatar engagement, we create cultural practices around pervasive media persona. Second, in order to frame agency, we must recognize a contextual use of media platforms.

Here, I look at how simulation may figure into a con-temporary understanding of copresence, followed by a discussion of experimental work with avatars and virtual reality (VR). The topics I address are verisimilitude of a simulation—how lifelike an avatar appears—and the issue of objectification (visualization) of subjective ex-perience. Additionally, I direct my attention to subjects' relationships to avatars (as opposed to subjects' mediated relation to each other *via* avatar).

In my assessment of VR research today, I find a con-nection between simulation and presence. In signifying presence, simulation does not represent a world apart, e.g., a map representing the empire, but, to the contrary, it rep-resents an aspect of the actual. In other words, researchers are using avatars and simulated environments to test real-world dynamics (around social status, identity markers, propensity for violence, and a host of other subjects). One of the sites of nascent research that I discuss explores the phenomenon of virtual impact on the real. Particularly in

experiments around modeling behavior, we are beginning
to see an actual influence of virtual figures on the behavior
of people.

Social Science of Presence

"If 'presence' is the 'sense of being there,' then 'copresence'
is the sense of 'being there together,'" writes Oxford Internet
Institute social scientist Ralph Schroeder.[6] Also known as
"social presence," the concept of copresence is really not so
very abstract if one thinks about everyday experience and
asks a question such as, "Can I tell how the other person
feels when I speak with her?" If this is a face-to face exchange, the answer is for the most part affirmative.

The human animal is very sensitive to deception, pain,
sadness, joy...in short, to the feelings of others.[7] As the
sociologist Erving Goffman discusses in his work on symbolic interaction, expression plays a critical role in understanding each other beyond the content of the words we
say.[8] Whether one chooses to respond appropriately or not
is a different question. All the information needed to make
a choice is there in a split second.

Now, ask the same question about a telephone conversation or an email exchange. How much expression is present in such a communication? How well does the medium
invoke presence of another? Beyond the face-to-face interaction, mediated communication tends to limit expression
even if it facilitates communication across geographical
distances. We get a portion of a person and his context: vo-
cal expression, background noise, a grimace or smile. We use
these mediated clues to form a full picture. In essence, we
are becoming expert at taking bits and pieces of people we
know well—a text message, a photo, a song—and transpos-
ing that into connected real-time presence. The importance
of copresence to the fragmentary relations we regularly
engage is the quality of a shared sensory experience of being
together. Though not the whole picture, these mediated
engagements provide actual shared moments.

On the subject of copresence, we must distinguish
between the affordances of different media platforms in

6. Ralph Schroeder,
"Copresence and Inter-
action in Virtual Envi-
ronments: An Overview
of the Range of Issues,"
*Presence 2002: Fifth In-
ternational Workshop*,
International Society
for Presence Research,
Porto, Portugal (Octo-
ber 2002): 276.

7. Ibid.

8. Erving Goffman,
*The Presentation of
Self in Everyday Life*
(Garden City, NY:
Doubleday, 1959).

9. Ralph Schroeder,
"Being There Together
and the Future of Con-
nected Presence," *Pres-
ence* 15, no. 4 (August
2006): 445.

order to properly frame the nature of mediation. To this end,
Schroeder draws a distinction between the *imagined* sense
of being there as we might experience with a book or a
movie and the sensory experience of being there together
that one might find with networked media technologies.
In different forms, mobile phones, immersive virtual
worlds (IVE), VoIP, and IM all provide a shared sensory
perception of connected presence. Schroeder writes on
this subject, "presence and copresence [do] not just mean
that people have an imagined sense of being there or being
there together, as, for example, in fiction, but [that SMS
and IM users] talk about their experience in terms of
sensory experience."[9]

Building on Schroeder's analysis, one might posit imagined presence as a space of self-direction; I am present to
my own thoughts and feelings. Sensory presence, on the
other hand, represents an actual relation with others; I
am present to *your* thoughts and feelings. If we attend to
a distinction between imaged and sensed presence in networked connections, we locate a critical factor in how we
communicate differently with the emergence of pervasive
media; we use it to create an ambient networked presence.
Rather than playing poor stand-in to real presence, networked media such as mobile phone and video chat—
through simulation—augment our lives.

Ambient Networked Presence
In everyday practice, I see people repurposing media
platforms to create what I am calling ambient networked
presence. By that term, I mean we share space, place, and
time via copresent media engagement. In effect, we turn a
video call, e.g., VoIP connection, or the exchange of media
artifacts, e.g., cell phone photos, into an "environmental"
portal. In such a schema, often the aspect of being connected is more important than the specific content exchanged.

For example, well-known blogger, Internet business
entrepreneur, and former Creative Commons CEO (named
the new director of the MIT Media Lab in the spring of
2011), Joi Ito writes of the "ambient virtual copresence"

that Skype, a VoIP application, enables. He portrays a
practice he and his friends have started where, by simply
keeping the Skype application open on the desktop, one
gets the audio (and sometimes visual) sensory experience
of the other person's day. "When I was in Helsinki," Ito
writes, "[then Nokia head of user experience] Matt Jones
also talked about how he kept Skype on all the time in the
background with his partner who was in another country
and felt her presence through the ambient sounds."[10] In
describing this practice, I am suggesting, Ito points to a
copresent media strategy. The VoIP application becomes
an open window through which Ito or the couple he describes creates a shared sensory experience.

I see this networked media practice as both a redirection
of what the Skype program ostensibly was made for (video
conferencing) and an affirmation of a mediated simulation
of presence as an actual presence. The purpose of the open
Skype window is not to speak or exchange particular information; rather the use of the application is an ambient way
to "spend time together" when people are locatively apart.

Similar to the Ito scenario, I interviewed a woman on
her Skype use with her husband, and she said that as a
couple they did not use the application for speaking with
each other but to make silly faces and nonsense sounds.
The couple did not, in fact, talk about anything (the typical
use of a telephonic connection). Rather, they used the networked connection to spend time together as if they were
face-to-face. We find a similar practice with long-distance
relationships between grandparents and grandchildren:
the VoIP window allows for an ambient engagement, without words or organized content as such (see figure 4.1).

I find in the practice of ambient networked presence
precisely this combination of technological affordance
(multimedia networked connectivity) and media agency
(people adapting the media platform to their ends) that
casts simulation as part of a X-reality spectrum: actual
experience is suspended between different points of everyday engagement that span physically embodied as well as
simulated proximity. Despite his visibility as a blogger, I

10. Ito posted these
comments to his blog
on December 24, 2003,
under the title "VoIP
enables ambient virtual
co-presence," <http://
joi.ito.com/weblog/
2003/12/24/voip-
enables-am.html>.

04:07 | Call with muttsenior

Ambient networked presence: Grand-
mother and grandson spend time
together over an open VoIP window.
Credit: B. Coleman

Fig.4.1

cite Ito's comments on copresent engagement as a reflection, in my view, of a quotidian use of media. The insight he provides into emergent practices of copresence is not based on technical expertise per se; rather, using a sense of cultural agency, he adapts networked media to make his environment more habitable. To portray his experience, however, he does avail himself of theoretical language, using the term "ambient virtual copresence" borrowed from media anthropologist Mizuko Ito (Joi's sister). My sense of this more formal framing of his insights is that Ito understands his media practice as similar to others'; what he describes is the emergence of a society change, not merely that of an individual user.

While working on Japanese mobile phone culture, Mizuko Ito developed the concept of "ambient virtual copresence." In explaining the term, she outlines the importance of "insignificant" or "not urgent" mobile messaging between close friends or couples, affirming the everyday and ambient aspect of these exchanges. Mizuko Ito and collaborator Daisuke Okabe write, "These messages are predicated on the sense of ambient accessibility, a shared virtual space that is generally available between a few friends or with a loved one."[11] Mizuko Ito's findings as well as those of media scholar Christian Licoppe and anthropologist Bonnie Nardi support my assessment of an ambient networked presence: when people connect via VoIP, IM, or text message, the value of that connection does not always rest in the information exchanged but rather in the fact itself of connecting. These are practices of networked presence above and beyond content transmission. In terms of media design, with a networked media channel such as Skype, or more recently FaceTime (an application that enables VoIP on mobile devices), we find media technologies that expressly support the transmission of human gestures. And, in term of agency, we use these channels to augment an intimate view of each other's lives by creating ambient environmental copresence.

In the 1990s, researchers on copresence primarily focused on the synchronous habitats of virtual worlds to look at the kinds of communication, community, and

11. Mizuko Ito and Daisuke Okabe, "Technosocial Situations: Emergent Structurings of Mobile Email Use," in *Personal, Portable, Pedestrian: Mobile Phones in Japanese Life*, ed. M. Ito, D. Okabe, and M. Matsuda (Cambridge, MA: MIT Press, 2005), 264.

12. Christian Licoppe,
"'Connected' Presence:
the Emergence of
a New Repertoire
for Managing Social
Relationships in a
Changing Communica-
tion Technoscape,"
*Environment and
Planning D: Society
and Space* 22, no. 1
(2004): 135–156.

13. Bonnie Nardi,
Steve Whitaker, Erin
Bradner, "Interac-
tion and Outeraction:
Instant Messaging in
Action," Proceedings of
the 2000 ACM confer-
ence on Computer
Supported Cooperative
Work (2000): 79–88.

collaboration that could be supported by a mediated proximity. We now find research on copresence across all forms
of networked media—mobile, IM, SMS, and VoIP. For his
work on telephony and SMS, Christian Licoppe has coined
the term "connected presence" to represent expressions of
ambient networked presence.[12] In her work on IM, Bonnie
Nardi registers a phenomenon of copresence in the format
of messaging across computers.[13] Their findings are representative of a network of scholars locating copresent events
across media practices.

In stories such as Joi Ito's or in the experimental research
of scholars such as Mizuko Ito, Licoppe, and Nardi, we find
instantiations of X-reality engagement where we fold connected presence into our daily lives. From these findings,
I conclude that the very nature of our communication has
changed. As we casually and ubiquitously create ambient
connectivity, we also engage in simulation of presence that,
for all purposes, relays an actual experience.

Walking the Virtual Gangplank: VR Lab
Stanford professor Jeremy Bailenson, an experimental
psychologist in the department of communication, asks me
and USC Annenberg School for Communication Professor
Dmitri Williams to step into a hole in the floor. We are
wearing a makeshift virtual reality (VR) headset that allows
the wearer to see the 3D image Bailenson's computer projects on the floor of the small gray office that is his Virtual
Human Interaction Lab. As the two guinea pigs, Williams
and I oblige by walking across a real plank then stopping
in the middle to jump into the projected virtual ravine
(see figures 4.2 and 4.3). I feel the earth rush up around
me as I experience my body plummeting down.

On the one hand, I am reasonably certain my body
has not left the office space or even left the solid floor. On
the other, I am definitely afraid of falling. I feel my body
hurtling through space, succumbing to the unavoidable
effects of gravity on bone. I expect the landing to hurt. Yet,
I have not gone anywhere. Bailenson has based nine years
of research on this kind of disjuncture that underscores the

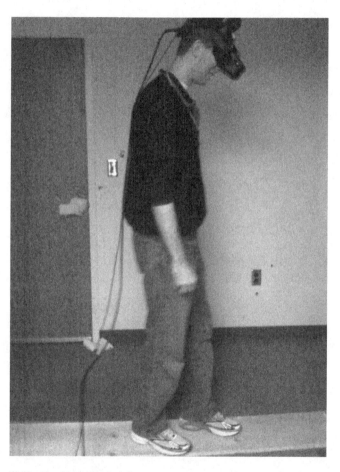

Walking the virtual gangplank: In a
VR research lab, a researcher walks a
real plank that appears above a virtual
ravine. Credit: B. Coleman

Fig.4.2

Leap of faith: Jumping into the ravine,
the author felt her body plummet
down. The VR lab focuses on the tension between the real, the simulated,
and the cross-wiring it affects in our
perception. Credit: B. Coleman

Fig.4.3

tension between the real and the simulated, and the cross wires it affects in our brains.

"Good," says Bailenson as I take off the helmet. "Most people hesitate."

"I knew it was not real," I say, mentioning out loud only half of the story. I had known it was a simulation, but it certainly felt real.

For the networked generation, we will only see an increase in the use of avatars and other forms mediation. VR researchers such as University of California at Santa Barbara social psychologist James Blascovich, Schroeder, and Bailenson try to gauge the nuance of human response to an acceleration of simulation. Their experimental work helps us to see two things: first, the growing presence of avatar interfaces in our daily lives and, second, the design of those interactions. Strictly speaking within the frame-work of HCI, an avatar is a "perceptible digital representa-tion" controlled by a human being.[14] But in looking at the spectrum of VR research, one finds in practice an open-ended definition of avatar, which includes among its forms telepresence (video), computer-generated images (2D and 3D animation), and even puppets.

Over the past decade, research on the use of shared virtual environments and avatar engagement has expanded to address a variety issues including identity, body image, behavior, and learning. We find simulation technologies being engaged well beyond the limits of HCI research and design, and, in fact, spilling into almost every activity for which we use computing. Additionally, VR research has a much broader mandate than when first initiated.

When the computer scientist Jaron Lanier coined the term "virtual reality" in the early 1980s it was the stuff of science and science fiction alike: fully immersive simulations that took banks of computers to run and for which the user would get suited up in interactive goggles, gloves, or even entire suits. The technology was rarified and expensive. The design focused on high-end, single users or small groups, which reiterated the exclu-sivity of the technology. Except for the stray hobbyist,

14. Jeremy Bailenson and Jim Blascovich, "Avatar," in *Berkshire Encyclopedia of Human-Computer Interaction* (Great Barrington, MA: Berkshire Pub. Group, 2004), 65-68.

15. *Toy Story* (1995, dir. John Lasseter, Pixar Animation Studios). *Final Fantasy: The Spirits Within* (2001, dir. Hironobu Sakaguchi, Square Company) the animated film based on the Japanese game series, pushed the outer limits of what could be represented as nearly photo real. It also pushed its audience away by wandering too far into the uncanny valley.

there was no such thing as peer-to-peer VR or a VR of personal computing.

For a period of time VR was famous, inspiring popular culture and serious research alike, and Lanier himself became a recognizable figure well beyond the reaches of the laboratory. For many years the push from industry and computer science has focused on creating a virtual human image with the greatest verisimilitude of representation. The goal was to make life on the screen almost as real as real life. Certainly, we have seen great strides in this direction. In the animation industry, the film *Toy Story* revolutionized how we saw 3D animation and goosed the film industry toward an animation renaissance.[15] However, the VR promise of a usable interactive platform, something that could be real time and reactive, not canned in its communication, never emerged.

There was no popular adoption because, technologically, there could be none. To this day, systems approaching a seamless representation of presence are still priced way beyond the reach of everyday users. To look like you have been beamed in from the holodeck, a fictive simulated reality room from the television series *Star Trek*, you have to approach the financial status of a rock star. As with many a technology that has been declared the next big thing, VR disappeared in a cloud of disappointment, ennui, and diminished expectations.

By the end of the decade, we were not walking around with 3D data goggles and gloves in the supermarket. We were, however, uniformly carrying cell phones and laptops, two forms of networked portable computing. What we see in the popular use of 3D simulation, in games and other avatar media, is that high fidelity—the endless quest for computer verisimilitude—may not be the most important factor in terms of the successful design. We are more interested in shared sensory experiences—the simulation of presence—than we are in a high-fidelity visualization.

Avatar Realism
One question that comes up in research and design of

avatars is: how real is real enough? In effect, how do we, the human participants, negotiate simulation? What do we need to authenticate, engage, and find meaning in experiences of simulation? Historically the perspective, from entertainment industry to military training, reflects the view that a serious use of avatars—for training, gaming, and so on—required as close an approximation of photo real as possible. If we know what the world looks like, it seems like common sense that we would try to reproduce an exact replica. Popular culture figures such as Hiro Protagonist in the novel *Snow Crash* or Neo in the film *The Matrix* offer great expectations of perfect simulation. As it turns out, designing the most realistic avatar has not proven to be the way to design the best networked experience.

In 1970, the roboticist Masahiro Mori framed the term "uncanny valley" to describe the effect of a robot that approaches a near human appearance but falls just short of achieving it.[16] Mori argued that a simulation that comes close to humanlike appearance produces a highly uncomfortable feeling for human viewers. More a qualitative term than an absolute value, the uncanny valley became a common conceptual reference with designers across fields of robotics, animation, and other forms of simulation. It marked the gulf between the made and the born as being most pronounced when there is the slight difference, not the great. Teddy, a teddy bear AI in the film *AI*, has a soothing and comic effect on its human users; while David, the synthetic boy who is the protagonist of the movie, makes everyone uneasy in his nearly perfect approximation of a real boy (dir. Steven Spielberg, 2001, Warner Brothers). Current research in avatar design rethinks the centrality of photorealism as the most effective way to design synthetic representation. We more strongly evoke mediated presence when we engage in human gestures, not life-like images.

Looking at this subject in a 2006 study, VR researchers Bailenson, Schroeder, Nick Yee, with computer scientist Dan Merget looked at the effects of realism in avatar form and behavior, finding that a combination of these two factors yielded the strongest results in test subjects.[17] In their use

16. Masahiro Mori, "The Uncanny Valley," trans. K. F. MacDorman and T. Minato, *Energy* 7, no. 4 (1970): 33–35.

17. Jeremy N. Bailenson, Nick Yee, Dan Merget, and Ralph Schroeder, "The Effect of Behavioral Realism and Form Realism of Real-Time Avatar Faces on Verbal Disclosure, Nonverbal Disclosure, Emotion Recognition, and Copresence in Dyadic Interaction," *Presence* 15, no. 4 (August 2006): 359–372.

18. As they state,
"Understanding the
relationship between
form and behavioral
realism is critical to
begin examining the
use of these new forms
of media." Ibid., 360.

of avatar faces, the team tested for several factors in user experience that included emotion recognition, copresence, and forms of verbal and nonverbal disclosure. The two charts they generated for the study gave a general picture of what avatars mean today within their limitations of representation (see figure 4.4). The study establishes a scale that moves from the highest representation of form and behavior to the lowest. Looking at the left-hand graph, which gauges real-time as opposed to recorded or static forms of avatars, one finds mirrors—the most commonplace form of reflection at the ultimate end of realism, where image matches behavior: your reflection looks and acts exactly like you. From there, in degrees of diminishing return, the researchers list live video feed, shadows, VR avatars, puppets, and so on.

In terms of the power of realism, the team places computer-generated avatars between shadows and puppets. The placement speaks to the mid-range status of computer-generated avatars, where they sit on the cusp of an image we comprehend as natural (and real), such as a shadow, and the markedly artificial image of a puppet. Most commercial VR applications tend closer to the puppet show, where the avatars are either fantastic alien creatures or simplified renderings of humans. In either case, in appearance alone, the standard avatar would never be mistaken for a real person. Once animated by their player, it is the combination of the avatar appearance and behavior that makes for the most evocative results.[18]

We can conclude from this schema that both the behavior and the formal aspects of an avatar—what it does and how it looks—affect the quality of communication. The richness of our experience online does not depend upon having a "pretty" face but rather the bundle of written, diacritical, and gestural behaviors and other artifacts that combine to represent us. As opposed to its appearance only, the power of an avatar comes from a network of associations including motion, cadence, and even suspension of disbelief. In other words, we animate our avatars, giving life to them by endowing them with meaning.

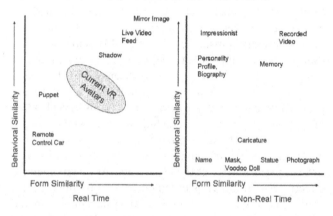

Representations of Human Beings (Avatars)

The effect of behavioral realism: In appearance alone, the standard avatar would never be mistaken for a real person. Once animated by its users, the avatar's appearance and behavior combined make for the most evocative results. Credit: Bailenson, Yee, Merget, and Schroeder, "The Effect of Behavioral Realism and Form Realism of Real-Time Avatar Faces on Verbal Disclosure, Nonverbal Disclosure, Emotion Recognition, and Copresence in Dyadic Interaction," *Presence* 15, no. 4 (August 2006): 359–372.

Fig.4.4

19. Before the age of the Walkman, a portable compact disk player, transistor culture had made music available away from the home. And the car stereo has always been the site of emotional, if not sonic, music fidelity.

20. Byron Reeves and Clifford Nass, *The Media Equation*.

In terms of simulation in general, we regularly augment the media object before us. For example, we would all be glad to have a perfect symphonic experience in Carnegie Hall, an architecturally designed setting for listening pleasure. Nonetheless, we will still listen to the cellist Yo-Yo Ma on tinny speakers or tiny earphones as the sound has shrunk to pocket size and portable.[19] We continue to enjoy Yo-Yo Ma or any other recording not only for the media content embedded on the vinyl, CD, or MP3, but also because of the memory of the pleasure we got from hearing a recording.

As with audio signals, so too with the rich media signals of current simulation: our imagination does a lot of work to fill in the gaps between objective experience of media content and perception. In other words, I do not have to mistake my cartoonish, 2.5 dimensional Habbo avatar (Sulake) for a real person to *engage* with my avatar as a representation of a real person. As discussed in chapter 2, Reeves and Nass have pointed out in their research that even rather shoddy looking avatars, in terms of realism of representation, can provoke human response.[20]

As VR research has suggested, visual realism does not determine success of a simulation. Other factors such as behavior strongly affect the experience. At this moment, effective avatar design is based on understanding a dual mode, where one relies on persuasive visual simulation and compelling simulation of behavior. The balance between the two depends upon the specific goals of the designer and the needs of the user. For example, playing a computer console game like Halo (Xbox) requires a high resolution, nearly photo-real 3D animated graphics, to simulate battlefield engagement. It also needs to have highly responsive behaviors in terms of player control of the avatar.

On the other hand, Club Penguin, the 2.5 dimensional web-based virtual world for children, thrives in its use of cartoon characters and very simple user controller events. The VoIP channel Skype would be an example of a third level of simulation; the digital video stream gives an exact rendition of image and behavior, but it is also marked with digital artifacts like scratchy sound and jumpy image. All three rest somewhere between the outer limits of visual realism, approaching the quality of a mirror, and the approximation of presence, the effect of being there where "there" is the purely computational and conceptual space of an online network. Given the scale of simulation, the question I ask here is how does the simulation affect the viewer?

Simulation as Objectification

One of the aspects of virtuality that we must keep in mind is that it objectifies the unreal. Things that are impossible, fantastic, or simply not yet made can be rendered before us in 3D simulation as if they were real. In effect, media can simulate and externalize internal states. In the history of media, we find a progression of objectification moving from the mechanical to the digital (and virtual) that marks changes in the way we perceive time, objects, and events. Photographs objectify our perception of reality, even as they can be manipulated.[21] To see an image of a movie star in a bikini or an alien landed on earth may not make the image a true representation of a fact, but it also may influence our opinion of the movie star's physique or the presence of aliens.

The notorious Rodney King video—the 1991 video taken by an observer of Rodney King, a black man, being beaten by white policemen in Los Angeles—was a visual trigger powerful enough to spark a riot. This widely circulated video, spread primarily by news media in this pre-web time, influenced the popular imagination to the point that when the accused police officers were found not guilty, the court of public opinion took action, and parts of Los Angeles burned.

From its origins, mass media has demonstrated the ability to influence opinion and to incite action. Objectification of perception—taking it outside of our internal view—can produce powerful consequences. When we look at this kind of objectification in regard to simulation technologies, we see strong potential for manipulating perception. Technically speaking, we are now in the position to model

21. Digital augmentation or touching up is common practice in fashion photography. In the 1980s, the public uproar over the naked image of actress Demi Moore on the cover of *Vanity Fair* grew from equal parts the titillation of the image (her body painted over with a suit) and the rumors floating around that the image has been stretched and digitally augmented to create a more striking image. The controversy was revivified in 2009, when the website Boing Boing posted an article that pointed to a chunk of flesh digitally removed from the actress' image on a *W* magazine cover. Xeni Jardin, November 17, 2009, "Was Demi Moore Ralph-Laurenized on 'W' mag cover, with missing hip-flesh?" <<http://boingboing.net/2009/11/17/demi-moore-is-ralph.html>>.

22. The name for this kind of knowledge acquisition is social cognitive theory, a concept developed by psychologist Albert Bandura in the 1970s. Albert Bandura, *Social Learning Theory* (Englewood Cliffs, NJ: Prentice-Hall, 1977).

23. Persuasive computing, also known as persuasive technologies, is designed to influence the behavior (or attitude) of a subject. It is a research and design category that includes aspects of psychology, HCI design, and computer-mediated-communication. Persuasive computing has been used in military application, user interface design, training, sales, and recently in health-care management. The ethics of what constitutes legitimate interaction and what constitutes coercion are neither well established nor universally applied.

24. Jesse Fox and Jeremy Bailenson, "Virtual Self-Modeling: The Effects of Vicarious Reinforcement and Identification on Exercise Behaviors," *Media Psychology* 12 (2009): 1–25.

virtual scenarios that put us in different outfits, bodies, or environments. As the testimony of the virtual cannibal supports (see chapter 3), our virtual actions result in actual consequences. Pervasive media presents a new form of simulation that differs from the tradition of mass media in scale (rather than massive and spectacular, we find ubiquitous and quotidian) and in kind (instead of one image being generated for all, we now customize simulation at the level of the individual).

With an abundance of avatars, we now have, in effect, an explosion of role models. As social cognitive theory asserts, much of what we learn comes from observing and mimicking the world around us; people learn by observing models.[22] VR experimentation extends social cognitive theory to virtual models. With new aspects of simulation, we must attend now to images, scenarios, and actions that are specified for us at a micro level. In light of this kind of persuasive computing, where the function of the program is to influence the subject's behavior, we must consider the limits of agency.[23] In effect, as subjects we can be framed within a simulation designed expressly for this purpose that uses representations of our face, our memories, and other renditions of our world. I discuss one such experiment below.

With graduate researcher Jesse Fox, Bailenson staged an experiment to gauge the impact of virtual behavior on actual behavior. "Behavioral modeling" is the clinical term for this kind of interaction. With the experiment, Fox and Bailenson tested the effects that an avatar may have on a person's self-image with regard to his or her physique. In their article reporting on the experiment, "Virtual Self-Modeling: The Effects of Vicarious Reinforcement and Identification on Exercise Behaviors," the researchers asked whether an avatar can motivate people to exercise.[24] And if the answer is yes, what have we learned about virtual behavior modeling?

Behavior modeling has a long history in experimental psychology. The term itself describes the process by which we are influenced by example. Our parents may model a

committed work ethic for us. An older sibling may model
rebellion. In the case of a VR modeling, the researchers
tested to see if virtual bodies come to impact flesh and
blood. The experiment focused on identification and behavior change—how much people associate themselves with a
model and to what degree that association affects behavior.
Fox and Bailenson tested this association using avatars that
were designed to resemble the test participants in varying
degrees, creating a visual likeness, and were also designed
to model different levels of activity, a behavioral model.

The test revolved around virtual motivation for physical exercise. The participants worked in three groups, one
in which an avatar running on a treadmill had the face of
the participant based on photographs rendered in 3D; the
second in which the avatar had the face of an unknown
person; and the third in which the avatar with the participant's face was seen loitering, meaning, nonactive. The
researchers found that after a twenty-four hour cycle, participants in the "self-running condition" showed higher levels of exercise in their real life than the other two groups.[25]
In other words, the active avatar with the subject's face
elicited the greatest response. (See figure 4.5.)

With the virtual exercise experiment, we see an example of powerful aspects of avatar use that we are just
beginning to recognize: avatars can influence people—
particularly when that avatar visually represents the subject.[26] Be the target weight loss or distance learning, there
is a growing body of research that suggests that virtual
models have the greatest impact when subjects see themselves as part of an experience and not simply watching
an experience. The shift from watching as a spectator to
engaging as a participant indicates that to see oneself virtually in a situation becomes a persuasive representation
of self. Of course, one must ask with this type of simulation: where is agency under such conditions? And, in our
exactitude of science, have we only returned to making a
more pointillist map of the empire?

The VR modeling exercise experiment concludes in a
relatively open-ended manner, finding that avatars may

25. Ibid., 13.

26. "Additionally, these results indicate that vicarious reinforcement of a 'self' model, as opposed to an 'other' model, sufficiently motivates exercise," Ibid., 17.

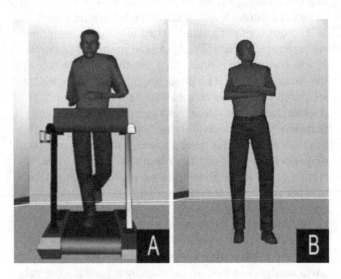

Modeling virtual exercise: Virtual tools
offer powerful forms of manipulation,
even at this early stage. Behavior, body
image, and memory all can be affected
by virtual stimulus. Credit: Jesse Fox
and Jeremy Bailenson, "Virtual Self-
Modeling: The Effects of Vicarious
Reinforcement and Identification on
Exercise Behaviors," *Media Psychology*
12 (2009): 1–25.

Fig.4.5

affect human users in a predictable manner given certain
conditions. In other words, research is still at an emergent
stage, and the results cannot be broadly applied to all avatar use. Nonetheless, initial findings in persuasive computing, like avatar self-modeling, are provocative enough to
warrant attention. Issues of privacy, manipulation, opacity
of system design, and participant control—to name a few—
come up very quickly. The most public examples we have of
engaging persuasive computing for "good" outcomes, such
as health care and weight loss, employ the same mecha-
nisms that can be applied to *any kind* of outcome, including coercion and misdirection.

With media technologies that augment presence—call
them VR in effect—we can find examples of agency where
we situate (and perhaps innovate) the manner in which
our avatars help make us present to others. The VoIP forays
toward an ambient networked presence are an example of
people designing their own forms of copresence with tools
at hand. We can also, on the other hand, point to media engagement that raises the specter of simulation as deception
and manipulation. For example, avatars engaged in a type
of persuasive computing where they wear our faces in order
to better influence our behavior. With pervasive media, we
find ourselves at a new crossroads in terms of simulation
technologies, where their very ubiquity has both rendered
them domestic and handy and also increasingly undetect-
able, where we can naturalize deception. Either direction of
media engagement, and they may not be mutually exclusive,
portrays a quality that is new to this generation of networked subjects. Our avatars simulate presence.

Practices of Agency
In retrospect, the inventor of virtual reality was right.
Lanier correctly predicted in the 1980s that VR would
be the future. It simply was not the future that had been
projected (see interview with Lanier at the end of the chapter). Looking at it under a particular light, VR has become
pervasive in computing and culture, as it is embedded in
the way in which we engage mediation. Instead of massive

processing power in an immersive laboratory setting, VR is a distributed network of granular, relatively inexpensive computer-mediated interactions.

The importance of virtual reality in the world did not arrive in high-tech full-body garb or even VR gloves, but in the humble wand of a Wii game controller. It has shown up in the mundane and ubiquitous—a sign of successful media and technology adoption. We see it in the way we avidly and easily engage gaming, video conferencing, social profiles, photo streams, and so on. As a culture, we live more extensively and, as I have argued, more comfortably with the world of simulation than previous generations; it is a key part of how we express ourselves.

In the future, avatars may be even better than the real thing—more human than human, or whichever science fiction slogan fits. But at the moment, and for the near future, we neither confuse the simulated figure for a real person— an *actual body*—nor do we mind, actually, that the virtual remains perceptually distinct. Our virtual persona work well enough for us in their imperfect forms, showing up where we cannot. They do so, I suggest, primarily as a form of augmentation—rather than substitution—of presence.

Jaron Lanier: The Popularization of Visual Communication

What follows is an interview with Jaron Lanier, a computer scientist, artist, and, recently, the author of *You Are Not a Gadget* (2010), a manifesto against network culture homogeny and objectification. Lanier was the central figure in the emergence of virtual reality in the 1980s. Technically and culturally, Lanier became the charismatic figure proselytizing a futurist vision of avatars as figures of deep communication and engagement. In his contributions to technoculture, Lanier defines himself as framing a new humanism (as opposed to techno fetishism). He discusses in the interview the aspirations of virtual reality and the qualities of the networked world we currently inhabit and also discusses current changes in network culture wrought by the proliferation of visualization technologies.

Location: Café, Berkeley California, February 13, 2008

INTERVIEWER: What are your thoughts on the current state of visual communication?

LANIER: If you go back twenty-five or thirty years, one of the hopes that a lot of us had for digital stuff is that there would be an expanded sense of what literacy means and I think that is actually happening. In the visual modality, I think there are a lot of people who are expressing themselves who would not have if they had been born in an earlier generation. That's not to say all is wonderful. But at least if you're designing your spot in Second Life or your MySpace page, there is an element of universal visual expression that I think is positive. There's a gender issue here too. It used to be more of a femmy thing to be visually expressive because you cared about fashion and interior design, and that was associated with femminess. Now its more gender neutral, and I think that is positive.

INTERVIEWER: As the science advisor to Second Life, what were you interested in doing?

LANIER: I was trying to push for getting over a threshold of a multiple-choice form of creativity. A multiple-choice form of creativity means, essentially, that you're assembling things from a kit, and the limits implicit in that. On the other side [of media design], you are forced to do things with enough open possibility that you don't quite know how to categorize what you [have done]. You escape ontology or predetermined ontology. And that is not a transition that Second Life achieved, although I believe it's achievable.

INTERVIEWER: What is your take on collaboration culture, the idea that crowd-sourcing and other forms of network group engagement make for better, smarter, outcomes?

LANIER: You have to be somebody in order to share yourself.

INTERVIEWER: The young people producing all these video iterations of themselves on YouTube, is this a process of becoming someone?

LANIER: Looking at teens on social networking sites, one observes a fairly wide range of behaviors. I think there's a switch that individuals have in their brain as to whether they are identifying with the world as an individual or as a group member. And I think that switch can go either way online and offline. Parenthetically, I think a group membership is potentially more dangerous than individual membership. It's a subtle issue and this is a whole long tail [discussed in his book *You Are Not a Gadget*]. I think what I am observing online is that for those kids who chose to use the Internet to help them be somebody, to be individuals, it actually works very well. And I think some of them are benefiting in ways that they would have found hard to replicate in the pre-Internet generation. But I think there's a larger number of kids who succumb to group identity and peer pressure. And those are doing worse. It's a little bit like the economic patterns in the U.S. Those who are engaged in terms of their sense of personhood are doing better than they would have and those who are not are doing worse. It's almost like there is a personality class system. I don't see a lot in the middle.

INTERVIEWER: What is the potential of populist virtual worlds like Second Life, Habbo Hotel, or World of Warcraft?

LANIER: You can think of virtual worlds and avatar design as explorations of pecking order in human society. I think there are different strategies. I can highlight two and I think they form something of a dipole. One of them is to seek out the safest, highest status avatar and that would be the slutty babe. All things being equal, the slutty babe has highest status and power. Far from having anything against the slutty babe avatar, I do have a bias against conformity. Let's compare that to another one, which is becoming creatively unique and contributing substantially [in such a] way that you cannot be dismissed. You become part of what makes the world livable for other people. As a strategy in life and in virtual worlds, I'd like to see people choosing more creativity of substance. Creativity of substance does not happen overnight. It requires work.

INTERVIEWER: How would you compare virtual reality to virtual worlds as they are now?

LANIER: To my mind the magic of virtual reality has only been experienced by a very tiny [number of] people with access to special labs. And that magic includes really physiologically taking on different avatars so your brain starts to believe in the homunculus of another being. The other thing is having an expressivity between people who are inhabiting avatars that really takes advantage of our cognitive powers. It's very powerful and astonishing. You're cutting closer to what the person is. Because ultimately whatever the avatar is does not matter so much, but something about their motions and the patterns of interaction between people is preserved. So there is a way in which the underlying cognitive being of people [is] preserved. And that's extraordinary. At what point can the designs [of virtual worlds and avatars] that go on become something startling? And that should happen if we are going to have an expressive medium.

Irving Wladawsky-Berger: Human Relations and Collaborative Tools
Dr. Irving Wladawsky-Berger is the chairman emeritus of the IBM Academy of Technology. For the past twenty years, he directed IBM's technical strategy and innovation initiatives. Wladawsky-Berger advocated for IBM's engagement with virtual worlds as a means to support the business's global employees as well as an innovation initiative. His advocacy for collaborative systems and technical interoperability are the focus of his comments here.

Location: Massachusetts Institute of Technology, Cambridge, MA, January 28, 2007

INTERVIEWER: What are the important things to work on for the next few years in network media?

WLADAWSKY-BERGER: Finding better tools for collaborating is critical. When you have a conference call it's 10 am to 11 am. You call and do business, bam, bam, bam. When you go to a physical meeting you discuss, how did the Red Sox do, and so on. It's almost like social foreplay, I don't know what the term is. When people in the global work force say they feel lonely, they are not lonely for a goddamn conference call. There is a human contact that is needed. We now have technology to build capabilities to help people feel happier in a very human sense. The people you work with—you have a relationship with them. They don't have to be friends, but you a have a relationship. And people want to be able to express that relationship. People want to belong and networked technology helps them belong.

X-Reality: A Conclusion

Pervasive Design: A Blast Theory Walk through Berlin
In October 2006, I am in Berlin walking into an art gallery
on the Fehrbelliner Strasse when my cell phone notifies
me that a text message has come in. I look at the screen to
learn that a group of us are assembling at a bunker to hear
a punk band play in ten minutes. I reply that I am on my
way. The art show in front of me is real, an exhibition that
merges principles of photosynthesis and electronics, but
the punk show to which I've promised to arrive will only
happen in the text message world of the alternate reality
game Day of the Figurines (see figure 5.1).

Alternate reality game (ARG) refer to a fictive or alternate narrative world overlaid on the real world. Often such
alternate realities engage multiple media formats, including mobile telephony, websites, and live-action play. ARG
is a type of pervasive game play that comes of age with the
experience of pervasive media use where the traditional
magic circle—the demarcation of where a game begins and
ends—becomes virtually unlimited. Portability of location-
aware devices, like many cell phones, the growing array of
cities with Wi-Fi hot spots, and the culture of always being

Day of the Figurines: Blast Theory walk
through Berlin with Alternate Reality
Game (ARG) played via text message
across the city, 2008. Credit: Blast Theory

Fig.5.1

networked all lend themselves to the fast ramp up of this style of gaming for both fun and serious ends. "Big Games," a related term, are a cousin to ARGs, using large systems like cities to play games. Another term that describes this sphere of media engagement is "mixed reality," which combines virtual and real environments for participatory play.

1. Although mixed reality remains a good descriptor, the term "augmented reality" has become the broadly used and thus canonical term by which people describe such forums.

Earlier that fall, the British art group Blast Theory had issued an open invitation for people to join them in Berlin to participate in a workshop of Day of the Figurines. Blast Theory makes ARGs, which the group calls mixed reality games.[1] "Games" may be a bit of a misnomer, considering the serious background the group holds in theater and research with the Mixed Reality Laboratory University of Nottingham. The group came to international attention in 1998 when it created Desert Rain, a mixed reality game played throughout London that rendered a critique of the Gulf War. Blast Theory creates immersive experiences that engage real-world and network events. Additionally, and crucially, audience participation represents the final element of their projects.

In the case of Figurines, Blast Theory took the city of Berlin as the actual playground and used a network of text messages to create a virtual overlay shared among the players. On the first day of the game, all the players met face to face in the art space Hallesches Ufer at the southern border of the city. Each player chose a figurine, a classic small, hard plastic figure often used in war games, then gave that figurine a name and a short biographical profile. Blast Theory took the figurine, now with name and identity, and input that information into the game database that allowed for real-time tracking of player interaction. The group then physically placed the plastic toy on a game board, a large grid on an even larger table that held 2D cardboard cutouts of the different sites that players would visit virtually, such as the bunker where the band would play.

A few moments after I received that first text message, my cell phone received another that read: "You are in a café. The people around you are laughing wildly..." I recognized it as the formulaic second person address of an interac-

2. Each generation, particularly since the invention of the Internet, can make this claim of an expansive development and adoption of networked media, with each generation eclipsing the one before it. In this sense, networked media technologies follow one of the laws of networks, i.e., they are ever emergent. For analysis of networked media of the 1990s, see Y. Ohta and H. Tamura, *Mixed Reality: Merging Real and Virtual Worlds.* (New York: Springer-Verlag, 1999).

tive game. Without further ado the game had started. The figurine on a board in a hall in Berlin became the avatar for my text message adventure overlaid on my real life journey through Berlin.

Everyday Life

The story of *Hello Avatar* is the growing power of the virtual in our everyday life. We move away from secure zones that demarcate the online from the real and speed toward a networked experience that merges layers of meaning and communication. Avatars, visual and gestural representations of ourselves across a network, have grown from the minimalist emoticon to ornate 3D creations that mimic real life. Similarly, our ability to represent information visually has greatly expanded along with the acceleration of real-time interaction. These factors affect how we use communication media. The work of this book is to describe how those changes are manifested.

The network theorist Albert-László Barabási names expansiveness as one of the key characteristics of a viable network; networks continue to expand, and, by necessity, the points of connection within the network also continuously increase. Thus, the logic of networks as applied to networked media indicates that we continue to expand sites of connection and, in my argument, sites of agency. We find today more platforms for remote or simulated real-time engagement than we have ever seen before. With each new media cycle, more media emerge.[2]

In thinking about the rise of the networked generation, what I have called this current moment of accelerated networked media adoption, I end the book with a discussion of platforms that describe a specific aspect of X-reality engagement: augmented reality as a design principle. If one engages across space, place, and time with X-reality platforms, then one can characterize X-reality design as that which adds an informational layer or communication extension to the world. As a mode of design, the technical and conceptual role of augmented reality is to emphasize a layered engagement in which multiple levels of presence and world may exist.

In its narrow sense, augmented reality, as a technique, refers to a visual or informational overlay that one can perceive (with the help of a viewing device) on top of objects and embedded in places in the physical world. The broader definition of augmented reality includes the multiple technical forms we engage to add information, connection, and increase presence in daily life. This includes platforms such as mobile telephony, real-time applications, social media, and locative media. What I am suggesting is that embedded in the practice of pervasive media is the experience of augmented reality.

As a technical field, augmented reality remains emergent, even though it is an old field as new media technologies go. In the late 1950s, cinematographer Morton Hellig invented the Sensorama simulator that augmented the visual experience of film with audio, smell, and motion. Computer scientist Ivan Sutherland's 1966 head-mounted display added to this history of visual augmentation immersive media design. By 1999, using a computer-vision-tracking technique, computer scientist Hirokazu Kato created the ARToolKit, which was an early version of augmented reality as informational overlay projected onto geographic sites.

From 2005 on, there has been tremendous growth in augmented reality design across sectors that include entertainment, information technology industries, property and engineering management, and architectural and industrial design. For my purposes here, I restrict the examples to quotidian engagement of augmented reality, where participants often create the form within which they participate or can generate content within it. My reason for this is to examine how augmented reality as a design principle of an X-reality generation is taken up in normal life. What I highlight here is a sector of X-reality design that purposefully exploits the experience of intersecting levels of information, engagement, and agency. To describe these platforms, we use a new vocabulary that speaks of alternate reality, mirror worlds, augmented reality in its narrow and broad framework, and the Internet of Things.

As I discussed above in relation to the Blast Theory project, alternate reality—named ARG in the game form—refers to a fictive world or event that people engage as an alternative to the real world before them. Real sites and material objects can be enlisted in the fictional world to move the narrative or game play foreword. Additionally, ARGs often engage transmedia tools, i.e., media across formats and platforms, to create an immersive experience across virtual, real, and imaged terrains.

In the past few years, we have seen significant growth in the use of ARG in gaming, advertising, and the entertainment industry. The first major media campaign to use an ARG was The Beast (2003), the pervasive game designed around the Steven Spielberg movie *AI*. A year later, I Love Bees (2004), which has become iconic in the ARG genre, led 600,000 players on a treasure hunt for information through the streets of Seattle and across media platforms such as broadcast television, the Internet, and local phone booths. With I Love Bees, lead designer Elan Lee, with his team at 42 Entertainment created the ARG as an experimental marketing campaign for Microsoft Company's Xbox game Halo II. In a sense, I Love Bees could be seen as one long ad for Halo II streamed across different platforms. In another sense, it expanded awareness of an immersive, highly participatory mode of engagement to a broader public that included those who played as well as those who heard about it.

Four years later Why So Serious (2007), the promotional ARG for *The Dark Knight* (2008) Batman film, engaged ten million users. The alternate reality story overlaid the events of a fictive Gotham City across globally dispersed sites. One could find videos of players in full makeup as Joker, the colorful villain of the film, posted from locations spanning Mumbai, Chicago, and the Great Wall of China. Designed by Jordan Weisman, the founder of 42 Entertainment, *The Dark Knight* ARG began its run a full year in advance of the film premiere, stirring up fan fervor. The company P, a Swedish production group, created a national scale with the ARG The Truth about Marika (2007) that played across television, online, and live action contexts. The production group created, with the support of national television and radio, what they termed "a fiction without borders" that wrapped the small country.

Outside of commercial enterprise, we can also track the growth of people creating inexpensive yet immersive engagement for one another. In the spring of 2007, Eyebeam Atelier, a new media arts organization, held a Big Games playoff with the help of New York University and professional design groups such as Playareacode. Participants came to play different games for a three day period in New York City, and then to gather in informal groups to discuss the proceedings. The projects of the Big Games playoff represented experimentation with the use of public space, civic engagement, and new ways to inhabit networked urban space as a collaborative platform. Additionally, the growth of independent ARGs (low budget and low tech) speaks to a form that has a much broader entry point than computer game design. For example, Must Love Robots, a New York-based ARG designed by Awkward Hug, had 300 players on a $3,000 game budget.[3] Games customized for a single player (with no budget) are now included in the emergent constellation of alternate reality engagement.[4] From the perspective of use and design, the evolution of ARG toward a recognizable cultural form points to an augmentation of reality that has begun to insinuate itself into the everyday.

Back in Berlin, during the crisp fall days when a group of us played through Day of the Figurines, there were several aspects of the game that did not work well. In terms of design, Blast Theory used the choose-your-adventure game format, where individual players would choose a text-based path along which to play. In this case, people were asked to choose their own adventures but in a virtual space occupied by other players. In terms of game play, this strategy is a bit like herding cats; everyone is running around but without a common purpose. Additionally, each unique path created by a player was telegraphed to the group via SMS, which contributed to a fragmented narrative of the events. Because of this procedural framing, at times the players fell out of synch

3. Must Love Robots ARG, Awkward Hug, <http://www.awkward-hug.com/>.

4. Experimental Game Dev Podcast Show, <http://www.indi-egamepod.com>.

5. Jane McGonigal, *Reality Is Broken: Why Games Make Us Better and How They Can Change the World* (New York: Penguin, 2011).

with each other, not receiving a message about whether another player was "present" in a location until that player has already left for another virtual destination or ended game play for the day. In general, Figurines was both too open ended (there were no clear rules or goals) and too narrow in its mode of interaction (each player was limited to a short set of commands and vocabulary for interaction) to work without player frustration. Nonetheless, despite the game's imperfections, I found myself very happy to have the virtual company as I made my way through the city.

Figurines offered my fellow participants and me a synchronous experience that wove its way into the routines of our days and nights. If one were indisposed, e.g., at work, in conversation, or sitting quietly, then pervasive engagement in this manner might be a terrific annoyance. But if players have the capacity to integrate this mode of ambient exchange into their day, the game play offers a new level of interest to daily activities. (I would suggest that the "capacity" to accommodate this form of engagement is a question of one's perception of time, time management, and valuation of the networked engagement and not simply a matter of "available" time in the day.) Instead of the ARG taking players away from real-world engagement, it can heighten the sense of being present. The sensibility of being part of something secret and compelling—part of a game—can contribute to general well being. As game designer Jane McGonigal has argued, in participating in an ARG one can feel more alert, involved, and empowered in the world because of the game layer that has been added to it.[5] In the broadest scope, the ARG experience is about augmentation. Whatever a player might be doing, this parallel world transpires across it.

Mirror Worlds
Like an ARG, a mirror world integrates a virtual layer of information into daily life. However, it does this by mirroring events in the world, as opposed to adding a fictive layer. A mirror world is a virtual site that reflects a real one. It not only mimics the physical aspects of a place but it can also highlight the human drama of a location. In other

words, a mirror world reflects real-world events. And, it illustrates how deeply we have already integrated networked media as a fact of life.

For example, the Associated Press (AP) ran a story on February 11, 2008, with the headline "Israeli Town Sues Google over Virtual Map."[6] The news agency reported that an Israeli town was in the process of suing Google, the giant web design company, for slander over a user posting on their map application Google Earth. The user, a Palestinian doctor named Thameen Darby, notated a section of the Google Earth map of the world. The Google Earth map provides satellite views of the world among other modes of photographic detail. People use it to previsualize travel to a place, to engage in modes of virtual travel, and to mark up the virtual map for other users to find personalized bits of information about a site. This is exactly what Dr. Darby did; he marked it up. But in this case, Darby wrote his note on top of an Israeli town called Kiryat Yam, stating that, in fact, the town had been built on the ruins of a Palestinian village.

The notation went up in a de facto public space (anyone can access Google Earth), which meant that all could read Darby's commentary, which was certainly political in its effect. As a territory, Kiryat Yam has a long-contested history and Darby wrenched open the debate anew. The AP article pointed out that the fight over Israeli-Palestinian territory, which is an old, terrestrial battle, now included a virtual wing. The actual conflagration took place not on the ground but around a mirror world. Google Earth offers a virtual reflection of real earth, and the history of conflict was transported into the virtual overlay. In effect, it was an x-reality moment that demonstrated the actual effect of virtual in the world. A mirror-world interlude such as the Google Earth conflagration tell us two important things about the state of augmented reality in X-reality design. First, we see ourselves increasingly playing with the informational structures that rest on top of the material world. Second, we invest actual interest in these informational layers, making virtual space an important part of the continuum with real space.

6. The AP story, "Israeli Town Sues Google for Slander," February 11, 2008, <http://en.wikinews.org/wiki/Israel_town_sues_Google_for_slander>.

7. Often augmented reality visualization is geolocative, which means the virtual image is tethered to a specific geographic location; one has to be locally and physically present to encounter the augmented artifact. Much pervasive media technology—the cell phone particularly—exhibits geolocative capability.

Halting State: Reality Hacking

If we can say that we apprehend reality through our senses, then augmented reality comes to us through the lens of computing devices—handheld networked machines. Augmented reality in its narrow definition, as already noted, is a visualization system that overlays virtual forms on top of what can be perceived normally. One uses an augmented reality browser, often bundled into the applications of a mobile device such as a phone or camera, to make visible virtual artifacts as one moves about in the world.[7] The current generation of augmented reality technology composes a blended landscape where we see an integration of virtual and real layers. I am suggesting that this augmented spectrum of perception speaks to an augmented sense of what we find to be actual.

In thinking about everyday practices of augmented reality, British author Charles Stross describes in his speculative fiction novel *Halting State* the ambient accompaniment of networked information overlaid on the brick-and-mortar experience of daily life. For Stross, a "halting state," a term taken from computability theory, stands for the tremulous and increasingly frequent intersection of the real and the virtual, where borders of meaning and agency cross. The novel centers on a crime perpetrated in a game world. Several Orcs (humanoid monsters from the *Lord of the Rings* novels by J. R. R. Tolkien) rob a virtual bank and actually upset the stock value of real businesses. Essentially the crime is a reality hack – the Orcs manifest their act in a virtual space, and yet the effects are felt in the financial sectors throughout the United Kingdom. In the novel a policewoman and game designer form a partnership to crack the case, enlisting augmented reality as a tool in finding the thieves across worlds real, virtual, and in between. The novel describes an X-reality neither very far-fetched nor far off, where we see informational constructs superimposed over the physical world.

Haunted Landscape: World Trade Center AR Browser

We see with augmented reality a kind of reality hack, where virtual things (object, acts, avatars) are exported to waking life. We find these porous boundaries not only in speculative fiction, but also in much of how we apprehend the world now. A video posted online by Wikitude, an Austrian augmented reality developer, shows a bustling New York City street through the screen of a mobile phone.[8] As the phone pans up, we see two virtual buildings filling the screen, and we realize that the site is lower Manhattan. The ghost impression we get, the augmented overlay onto the real, is a simulation of the Twin Towers, bombed to the ground on September 11, 2001 (see figure 5.2). The towers are rendered as simple grey rectangles without a great deal of photo-real detail. Nonetheless, the effect of placing the towers back in their original location is haunting. In "geo-tagging" the augmented reality visualization, i.e., making the networked media specific to that site, the designers use the situated context as a powerful aspect of networked media design. The Wikitude video demonstrates two impulses at play with the use of augmented reality. On one hand, the media design company taps public memory to catalyze interest in a new technology. Augmented reality offers a new way to share and commemorate. On the other hand, the Wikitude video borders on poor taste, building a marketing pitch on the back of trauma. Both of those potentials of the media technology are attached to it from the outset.

Moving out of the box and into the street, augmented reality is a shared experience and a ubiquitous one. As opposed to the contained exchanges of telephone or text, augmented reality behaves more similarly to a broadcast medium like radio. In this light, media futurist and design geek Bruce Sterling has predicted that augmented reality, for all its playful wonder, will congest the world with 3D spam (a geolocative information trash).[9] It is precisely this question of how we engage the next level of pervasive media that we are auditioning now both technically and culturally.

Both in science fiction and media design, we find investigations that target a borderland between virtual and real contexts. Like Stross, author Vernor Vinge, in the novel *Rainbows End*, forecasts in obsessive detail a world in which we translate with our *biologically embedded* media

8. The Wikitude video of WTC AR, "World Trade Center: Its not there but its there [sic]," went up on YouTube on October 06, 2009, with the following note: "WTC— A symbol for what man can do. WTC is the first 3D model added to Wikitude." <http://www.wikitude. org/>; <http:// www.youtube.com/ watch?v=V8D5wB Eiwgk>.

9. In his keynote address on augmented reality to the Dutch augmented reality browser company Layar, Sterling describes the good, the bad, and the ugly of the nascent industry. He saw the marvelous effect of augmented reality as real-world, real-time interaction, and the inevitable dangers from spam to trolls to security breaches. Bruce Sterling, "At the Dawn of the Augmented Reality Industry," hosted by Layar, August 17, 2009. <http://layar.com/ video-bruce-sterlings-keynote-at-the-dawn-of-the-augmented-real-ity-industry/>, posted August 20, 2009.

Halting state: Wikitude's augmented
reality view of the ghostly Twin Towers.
Credit: Wikitude

Fig.5.2

readers the crackling skein of augmentation that is taken as part of everyday life. Vinge sees a near future world in which we play with the air, commanding input/output feeds with the slightest gesture. Back in the world of actual technologies, a project such as SixthSense, the gestural computing system out of computer scientist Pattie Maes' Fluid Interfaces group at the MIT Media Lab, is a prototype for precisely this kind of invisible interface between our augmented world and us. Augmented reality is a pervasive medium in the most literal sense of the term, in that it pervades lived experience and embodied spaces.

Internet of Things: Pachube
Like augmented reality design, the Internet of Things (also known as social objects) puts into play the relation between the physical and informational world. As I have discussed in chapter one, the Internet of Things is a broad category for media technology designers creating objects, actions, and capacities that are tethered to a network; we have started to create sense-able objects for an increasingly linked-in physical world. As an example of Internet of Things design, Pachube offers a kind of do-it-yourself ubiquitous computing, where real-world objects, actions, and capacities can be sensed remotely across the platform. It forecasts change in networked interaction where agency exists not only on the level of information exchange but also in relation to objects and actions.

Pachube is a software platform that works as a networked patch bay. Historically, a patch bay was a physical console through which different lines, such as telephone connections, could be "patched in;" it served as a hardware dock by which a network of connections could be made. A virtual instrument, Pachube works in the same manner conceptually by connecting environments. An application designed by UK architects Haque Associates, Pachube tests modes of sharing that link not only people but objects and actions as well.[10] Pachube captures sensor input—information about a physical, sense-able place—and serves this information as output data to remote sites. In other words, people post

10. Its technical framework is an open build that users can fit to their own needs. Pachube uses industry-standard protocols of Extended Environments Markup Language (EEML) and an EEML Processing library and works with Industry Foundation Classes (IFCs), <http://pachube.com>.

11. "Real-Time
Radiation Monitoring
in Japan—Internet
of Things in Action,"
Monday, 21 March 2011,
<http://blog.pachube.
com/2011/03/real-time-
radiation-monitoring
-in-japan.html>.

locally-based sensor information and Pachube pushes it toward a network of other participants. The platform connects real places and things using a virtual network. For example, Natural Fuse, a network designed for carbon emission offset, is a Haque studio project that demonstrates Pachube's augmented reality design capability.

A Pachube customization, Natural Fuse links a group of carbon-producing computers with an array of plants, offsetting the emissions (see figure 5.3). For Natural Fuse to work, participants have to agree to the ground rule that they will not use their computers beyond the amount the plants can match with oxygen in aggregate. Once that is established, a balance of oxygen from hours of low computing can be stored in the system to be used against periods of high computing. Both by automating greater energy efficiency and making habits about energy use transparent to the people on the network, Natural Fuse patches in objects, information, and actions across its network. At its core, the platform application performs an X-reality function; as a virtual instrument, it links events in the material world.

Another recent use of the platform has been for emergency situations. In March 2011, after the catastrophic events in Japan involving earthquake, Tsunami, and the destabilization of a nuclear reactor, a loose affiliation of media designers used Pachube to aid in the crowd sourcing of real-time radiation monitoring in Japan. Essentially, the designers customized Pachube to map radiation data that was supplied by hundreds of people locally, creating a rapid and accurate mapping of the disaster.[11] With applications such as Natural Fuse and the Japanese crisis mapping, I am suggesting that Pachube, as opposed to being an exception, represents an emergent mindset in media technology design that looks to augment reality in a meaningful way for everyday engagement.

The significance of this shift in the technical design of systems is profound. We can augment our lives to help us take better care of our health (medical, health, and fitness systems), better care of our environment (pollutants, recycling, waste systems), and keep better track of where

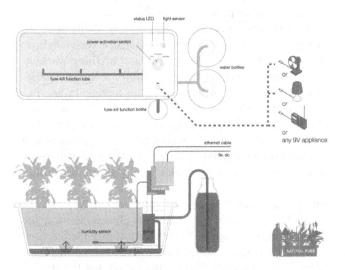

status LED   light sensor

power-activation switch

fuse-kill function tube

water bottles

fuse-kill function bottle

or

or

or
any 9V appliance

ethernet cable

9v. dc

humidity sensor

NATURAL FUSE

X-reality patch bay: Pachube platform
connects real places and things using
a virtual network. Natural Fuse uses
Pachube to create a symbiotic circuit
between carbon-producing computers
and plants that offset carbon dioxide.
Credits: Haque Associates

Fig.5.3

our stuff is (property, assets, and other types of systems management). Designers working in this field such as Timo Arnall, Julian Bleeker, John Thackara, and Hiroshi Ishii, early leader on tangible media—all think about making objects or systems of collaboration "smart" by putting things and people in a networked relation. The idea is that local knowledge and resources should be supported and changed by the real-time presence of a network. In effect, if our objects become smarter, then we too can behave in a smarter way, as participants in said system.

As with other practices of augmenting reality, with the extension of mediated reach comes, also, an extended consequence of action. If with the Internet of Things we augment reality to include expressive objects, then we must equally consider the other side of this augmentation. In effect, how might we think of agency in a world in which objects are also "smart?" And, at a more localized level, at what point do our "smart" houses, cars, and appliances begin to report on our behavior? Issues of privacy as well as cultural bias come up very quickly. We must be cognizant of when technologically "smart" might mean socially or culturally stupid. Designing for greater connectivity can also translate to a greater surveillance of objects, actions, and people. I argue for an understanding of extended agency as a central consideration of pervasive media design and engagement. I do so with the stipulation that the *situated context* of networked media informs its actual use. In my view, the best form of a "smart" system would be one in which a participant comprehends the technical affordances and recognizes how he or she might affect this system. In short, participants must see themselves as agents in a way that informs the situated nature of a system, as opposed to having our objects inform on us.

This is not a utopic vision based on total transparency of media technologies or full media literacy of participants. Rather, my constrictions recognize the actual dynamic modes in which people engage, adopt, and adapt networked media technologies. As a group, the projects I discuss here represent early twenty-first-century experiments in X-reality design; all enact an experience of the actual that underscores the agency of the participant. We find everyday engagement of an augmented reality across a spectrum of media platforms and sites of agency. Either as designers or participants, in one form or another, people are making their networked worlds inhabitable. In other words, the makers are making themselves at home by way of their avatars.

Pandora's Box: The Blue Face of the Future
In his 3D feature film *Avatar* (2009), Director James Cameron invokes a concept of avatar both ancient and futurist. The film portrays a group of scientists, who like gods of technology, use their powers to transpose their subjectivity into avatars of an alien race, the Na'vi. The audience watches the journey of Jake Sully, a paralyzed soldier from Earth, who finds his way back to physical and psychic wholeness by merging his persona with a Na'vi body; by way of future technology, he is incarnated as a native hero. Pervasive media, in this science fiction tale, takes the form of full body immersion, where external markers of computers, screens, and gadgetry are jettisoned for the wrapper of a new body. The narrative arc of *Avatar* describes Jake Sully's use of an embodied form of mediation to find his way back to engagement in the world (and, of course, a little love along the way). We can understand his avatar, then, as a figure of connectivity—a nodal point enabling connections across platforms. As I have framed the term, avatar demarcates a point of connection not only across technological networks but also connections of self to others and to world. I underscore this play between technological affordance and agency by returning to the example of *Avatar*, with a focus on the Na'vi. Their job in the film, as such, is to illuminate a concept of avatar outside the constructs of science.

Bathed in the tropical flora and fauna of the alien planet Pandora, the audience meets the Na'vi, a society of blue skinned warriors, in their native setting. In a parallel gesture to Jake Sully's technological connection to his avatar (though not equally prioritized in the film), the

Na'vi connect the tips of their tails to the buds of vines around them, and, in that manner, they interface directly with their deity, the earth spirit of Pandora. Thus, with the Na'vi, the viewer sees another variation of avatar: the people are a face of the god.

The narrative and the immersive design of *Avatar* work together to send a message about our current moment of pervasive media. From the perspective of Jake Sully, the protagonist, his avatar is not a public face or a mask but the idealized version of the self. For the Na'vi, being connected is the nature of being itself. Certainly, the film portrays an unabashedly romantic vision of the Na'vi—one in keeping with a long tradition of "noble savages" who save the Western world from itself. I would suggest though, as counterpoint, that the desire for a networked self that is, somehow, a true self can be found across cultural narratives. As I have discussed (see chapter 1), we find the fantastical idea of presence through mediation in the mythological tales of Lord Krishna, the blue-faced hero who embodies the god Vishnu in avatar form. (Krishna is one example among many of the avatar as figure of mediation.) The success of Avatar as a film is its ability to tap into a technological futurism and an epic, ancient narrative of heroes who channel the highest spirits. As a fiction, *Avatar* promises that we can be our best selves in avatar form.

As the next cycle of media technologies—what I have called pervasive media—enters the culture, we also find a promise of transformation through mediation. It is a promise implicit in the technical design of the media. But also, importantly, it is a cultural promise, a discourse of networked subjectivity, that frames the early twenty-first century. As opposed to the life of gods and heroes, I have framed this transformation in terms of an everyday experience of augmented reality and extended sites agency. In the combination of the two, I find an emergent practice of X-reality engagement. In this sense, our trajectory with networked media is similar to Jake Sully's alien encounter, where pervasive media aids one in recognizing self as agent: we have capacity to effect change across our worlds.

Before she became a planet in the science fiction pantheon, in Greek mythology Pandora was the first woman, and,
like the Bible's Eve, she was formed directly by the hands of
the gods. Pandora comes into the world with a box (or a jar
in the Greek) that contains the plagues of the world, but also
hope. When she scatters the contents of her jar, according
to the poet Hesiod, "Only Hope was left within her unbreak-
able house."[12] In keeping with this tradition, we still find
new technologies in the form of a Pandora's box. With these
tools in our hands, we can unleash plague upon our world
or we can harness them for good. As a networked global
culture, we now have the job to negotiate, cajole, charm, and
demand what that "good" might look like at the level of the
locally situated and the interconnected.

These early days of X-reality use and design beckon
with an offer of god-like powers. We can touch remote
objects. We can appear with different faces. We command
time and space. Historically, with each disruptive technology—each new form that strongly affects the world—one
can make a similar claim. As with the arrival over a
hundred years ago of the railroad, the telegraph, and the
telephone, with the advent of a pervasive media network,
one sees transformation at a global scale. As I have argued throughout this book, the critical change in the shift
from early Internet adoption to pervasive media is the
extended scope of human agency. The increased ability to
meaningfully engage and impact the world in which we
live—agency in short—is the disruptive technology of our
time. This generation of networked media engagement is
already underway. From the niche users of early virtual
worlds to the broad adoption of real-time platforms today,
we see a shift in media use that reflects an expanded view
of self and agency beyond physical boundaries. The deep
change we are making—sometimes we drive it, and other
times we move along with it—speaks to a mobile, pervasive, and powerfully networked experience of the world.

12. Hesiod, *Works and Days*, trans. M. L. West (New York: Oxford University Press, 1999), 168.

Procession of
Avatars

The history of "avatar" and the evolving meaning of that
term span millennia. It originates in the ancient Sanskrit
language of Hinduism, where it meant the god descending into a terrestrial form (see chapter 1). In the following
series, the first image shows the gods Vishnu, Brahma, and
Shiva with the multiple faces of their avatars. The second
image depicts Vishnu in his dwarf avatar. Over time, in
the English language, "avatar" came to stand for a mode of
allegory—figural representation. And now most recently,
in the wake of the creation of computer-generated interactive figures, the avatar is the digital embodiment that
represents us in a networked forum. Over the course of this
book, I argue that our avatars take critical shape in text,
graphical, and other communicative forms. It is not only
the visually expressed body that creates our persona as
networked subjects. With that said, the following group of
images represent a fast forward through the visual history
of avatars, where we find figures that embody various epis-
temological stances, from the spiritual to the technological.

Following the images is an X-reality timeline that tells
a separate but coinciding history of virtuality and mediated

1. Two excellent sources on the history of war machines and simulation are Manuel De Landa, *War in the Age of Intelligent Machines* (New York: Zone Books 1991), and James De Derian, *Virtuous War* (New York: Basic Books 2001).

presence. Avatars and virtual worlds can exist without each other. However, I make the point in the argument of the book and with the graphic support of the timeline that we glean a richer understanding of avatars and the spaces of mediation by embedding distinct instances in a history of technology and cultural engagement. In the timeline, I focus on the history of computer-simulated images and real-time interactive platforms, such as virtual worlds. I use the term "X-reality" to address the broad forms of simulation that comprise our technological, mythological, and media cultures. This includes aspects of the extended military play with technologies of simulation, beginning in the timeline with flight simulation around the turn of the century, but certainly that history traces back to the invention of warfare as such.1 But I include in the timeline other sites of simulation that I believe need to be read together as a whole, as we see them, driving this emergent experience of pervasive media. I include networked games, speculative fiction, mobile devices, events in media history, and participatory platforms as part of the X-reality platforms described. The timeline in its printed form is one iteration of what I believe must be a collectively generative history. The online supplement to the book connects the reader to various communities and resources where this media archeology takes place . . . and history is still being made. Please go to helloavatar.org to access the media hub.

B. Coleman
Research assistant: Jaroslav Svelch

Figure I.1 Faces of the gods: "Worship of Vishnu, Brahma, and Shiva," early twentieth-century painting, Indian, ink and opaque watercolor on paper. In Hinduism, the reincarnation of three major gods plays a recurring theme. In the figures of Brahma, Vishnu, and Shiva pictured here, one sees multiple views of their avatar faces. Credit: Harvard Art Museums/Arthur M. Sackler Museum

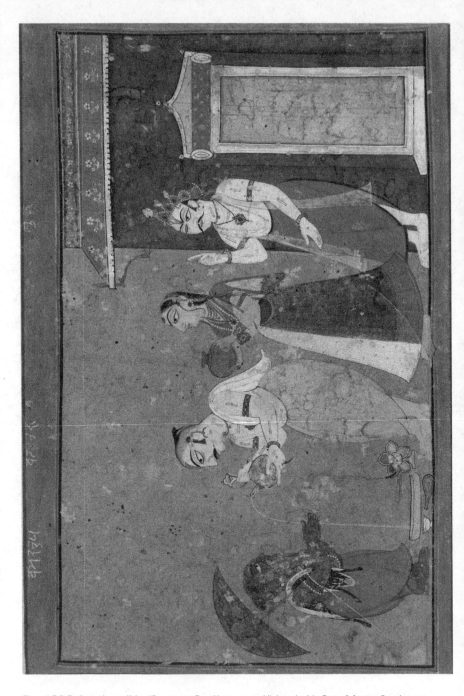

Figure I.2 Before the guilds: "Devotees Pay Homage to Vishnu in his Dwarf Avatar," unknown artist, ca. 1720, Indian, eighteenth century, ink, opaque watercolor, and gold on paper. Vishnu appears to his followers as a dwarf avatar. Contemporary fantasy role-playing games such as the paper and dice Dungeons & Dragons or the simulated online World of Warcraft also offer dwarf avatars among the roles players may choose. Credit: Harvard Art Museums/Arthur M. Sackler Museum

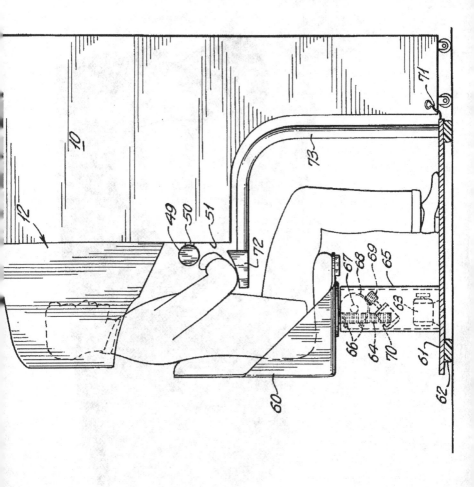

Figure I.3 Sensorama Simulator patent drawing, M. L. Heilig, 1962. The Sensorama Simulator (1957) created a 3D motion picture with immersive sensory stimulus that included stereo sound and vibration. Credit: M. L. Heilig

Figure I.4 Flight simulators use visual environment element: F-16 Egypt unit training device. Pioneered by the American engineer Edward Link, the flight simulators of the 1960s began to use CCTV systems and then computer graphics to create precise and realistic 3D virtual space. Credit: Link Simulation & Training

Figure I.5 Nice day for a quest: Habitat. In 1985 Chip Morningstar and Randall Farmer developed for LucasFilms a multiuser game called Habitat that played across a 2400-baud modem on a Commodore 64 console. With its 8-bit players, Habitat was the first graphical multiuser dungeon (MUD). Credit: LucasFilms

Figure I.6 Memory palace: Opening day at Palace in Wonderland, 1996. The Palace was a graphical 2D chat environment with user-created avatars. It was part of the emergent avatar culture of the 1990s. Jim Bumgardner developed the platform for Time Warner Interactive. Credit: original artwork by Cybrea

Figure I.7 Avatar rising: In Richard Garriott's single-player role-playing game Ultima IV: The Quest of the Avatar (1985), the term "avatar" was first applied to a virtual persona. The player sets out on a quest to become the Avatar—the spiritual leader of people. Coincidentally, Chip Morningstar of the Habitat team started using the word "avatar" to describe the online persona of that multiplayer game. Credit: EA

Figure I.8 Full metal jacket: Full Spectrum Warrior (2004) is a 3D tactics videogame developed for training of U.S. Army soldiers by the Institute for Creative Technologies with Pandemic Studios, and then published for consumer use by THQ. Part of a long line of simulation for military training, the game offered an immersive virtual world. THQ made the game a free download in 2008. Credit: THQ

Figure I.9 Randomize me: Sulake's Habbo Hotel avatar selector allows players to customize their virtual world persona; Sulake randomized that selection process for its massively popular 2.5D youth world. Credit: Sulake

174

Figure I.10 Beautiful girls virtual world: Portrait of avatar Aimee Weber of the artists' series "The 13 Most Beautiful Avatars," by media artists Eva and Franco Mattes. The visual impact of Second Life avatars, the ability to customize and beautify within a 3D adult virtual world, is part of the allure of the platform. Credit: Eva and Franco Mattes

Figure I.11 Multiverse, Inc. (2005) created a virtual world middleware kit where designers could create their own worlds. The screenshot comes from LunarQuest, a multiplayer game world set on the Earth's moon developed by The RETRO laboratory with Multiverse tools. Credit: Lunar-Quest, The RETRO laboratory

X-REALITY
TIMELINE

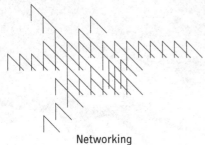

Networking

Ideation, immersion, play

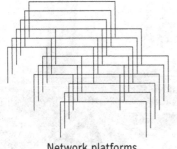

Network platforms

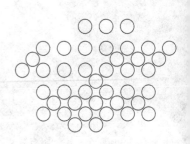

Virtual objects, visualization

3D technology

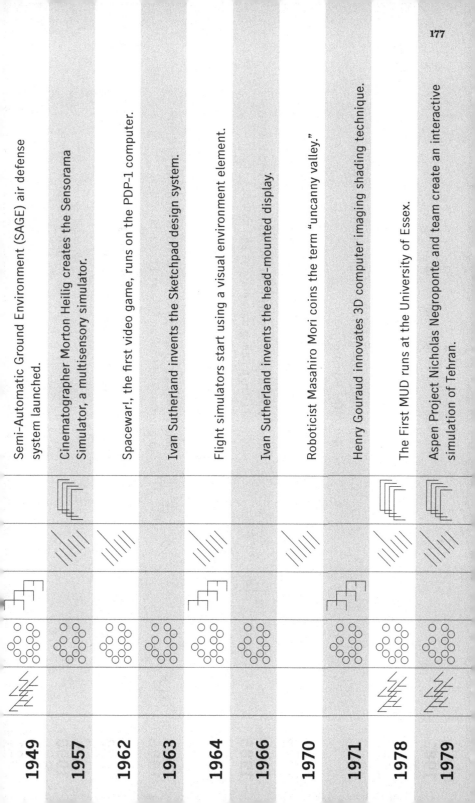

1949 — Semi-Automatic Ground Environment (SAGE) air defense system launched.

1957 — Cinematographer Morton Heilig creates the Sensorama Simulator, a multisensory simulator.

1962 — Spacewar!, the first video game, runs on the PDP-1 computer.

1963 — Ivan Sutherland invents the Sketchpad design system.

1964 — Flight simulators start using a visual environment element.

1966 — Ivan Sutherland invents the head-mounted display.

1970 — Roboticist Masahiro Mori coins the term "uncanny valley."

1971 — Henry Gouraud innovates 3D computer imaging shading technique.

1978 — The First MUD runs at the University of Essex.

1979 — Aspen Project Nicholas Negroponte and team create an interactive simulation of Tehran.

178

1981 — *True Names* by Vernor Vinge is published.

1982 — William Gibson coins the term "cyberspace."

— Israel develops the first modern unmanned aerial vehicle (UAV), MQ-1 Predator.

1984 — *Neuromancer*, William Gibson's first cyberspace novel, is published.

1985 — Jaron Lanier popularizes the term "virtual reality" and founds VPL Research, building data goggles and gloves.

— The term "avatar" is first applied to virtual persona; Ultima IV, EA.

1986 — Habitat, the first graphical virtual world, is launched by Chip Morningstar and Randall Farmer, LucasFilm.

1989 — SimCity, a personal computer game designed by Will Wright, casts its players as virtual urban planners.

1990 — The first MOO server is running, written by Stephen White.

1991 — *Synners*, an augmented reality novel by Pat Cadigan, is published.

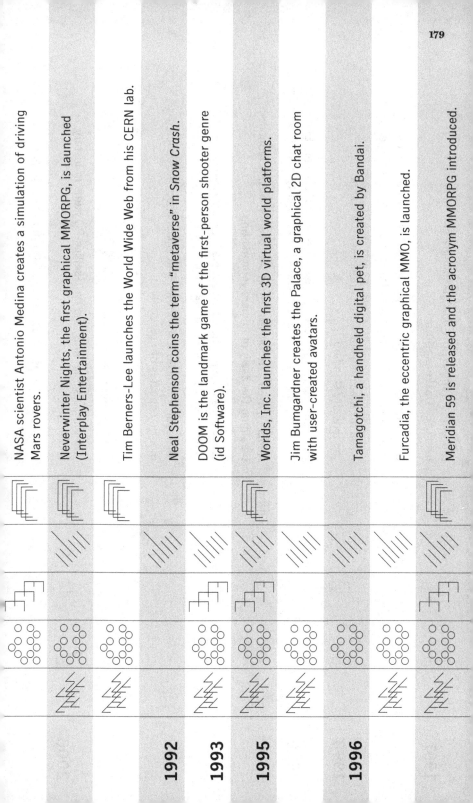

179

NASA scientist Antonio Medina creates a simulation of driving Mars rovers.

Neverwinter Nights, the first graphical MMORPG, is launched (Interplay Entertainment).

Tim Berners-Lee launches the World Wide Web from his CERN lab.

Neal Stephenson coins the term "metaverse" in *Snow Crash*.

DOOM is the landmark game of the first-person shooter genre (id Software).

Worlds, Inc. launches the first 3D virtual world platforms.

Jim Bumgardner creates the Palace, a graphical 2D chat room with user-created avatars.

Tamagotchi, a handheld digital pet, is created by Bandai.

Furcadia, the eccentric graphical MMO, is launched.

Meridian 59 is released and the acronym MMORPG introduced.

1992

1993

1995

1996

180

1997

Diary of a Camper, the first machinima film, is made using the Quake platform.

Ultima Online is released, the MMORPG whose commercial success proved the viability of the genre (lead designer: Ralph Koster).

1998

Maya 3D modeling software is released, to become the industry standard.

1999

EverQuest fantasy MMORPG is launched by Sony Online Entertainment, the first MMORPG to surpass the popularity of Ultima Online.

Neopets, a 2D cartoon virtual pet website for kids, is launched, heralding the dawn of immersive marketing.

Whyville, a 2D educational virtual platform for tweens, is designed by J. Bower of Caltech.

Microsoft's MMORPG Asheron's Call is launched, introducing monthly updates of new content.

Hirokazu Kato develops ARToolKit, HITLab.

Will Wright's The Sims, the best-selling PC game in history, is released.

2000

The popular teens' virtual world platform Habbo Hotel starts in Finland.

2001

RuneScape, a free java-based MMORPG, launches.

FunCom starts Anarchy Online, the sci-fi MMORPG.

Dark Age of Camelot launches, Mythic Entertainment's MMORPG based on Arthurian legends.

Friendster starts the social networking trend.

2002

Square Enix launches the Final Fantasy XI MMORPG.

There, an avatar-centered 3D virtual world platform, is released.

EVE Online, a 3D science fiction trading and combat MMO, is the creation of the Icelandic company CCP Games. EVE players can organize themselves into corporations, complete with CEOs and shareholders.

2003

Project Entropia, a MMORPG/virtual world hybrid, is released.

Linden Labs' Second Life, a 3D virtual world platform, launches.

del.icio.us social bookmarking system opens.

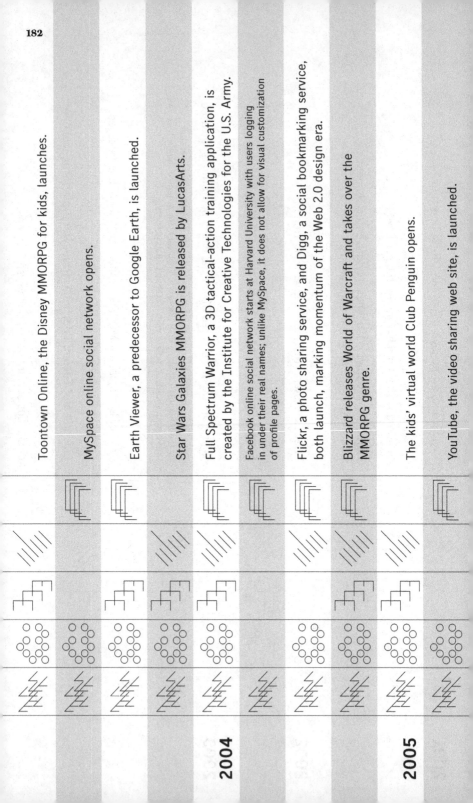

Toontown Online, the Disney MMORPG for kids, launches.

MySpace online social network opens.

Earth Viewer, a predecessor to Google Earth, is launched.

Star Wars Galaxies MMORPG is released by LucasArts.

Full Spectrum Warrior, a 3D tactical-action training application, is created by the Institute for Creative Technologies for the U.S. Army.

Facebook online social network starts at Harvard University with users logging in under their real names; unlike MySpace, it does not allow for visual customization of profile pages.

Flickr, a photo sharing service, and Digg, a social bookmarking service, both launch, marking momentum of the Web 2.0 design era.

Blizzard releases World of Warcraft and takes over the MMORPG genre.

2004

The kids' virtual world Club Penguin opens.

YouTube, the video sharing web site, is launched.

2005

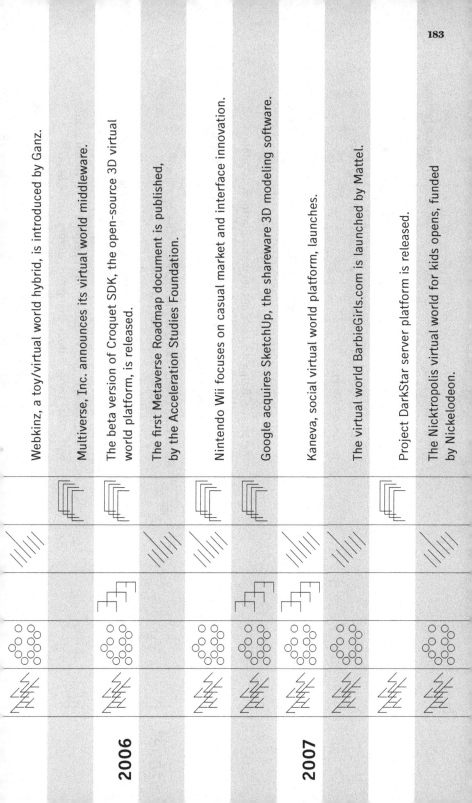

Webkinz, a toy/virtual world hybrid, is introduced by Ganz.

Multiverse, Inc. announces its virtual world middleware.

The beta version of Croquet SDK, the open-source 3D virtual world platform, is released.

The first Metaverse Roadmap document is published, by the Acceleration Studies Foundation.

Nintendo Wii focuses on casual market and interface innovation.

Google acquires SketchUp, the shareware 3D modeling software.

Kaneva, social virtual world platform, launches.

The virtual world BarbieGirls.com is launched by Mattel.

Project DarkStar server platform is released.

The Nicktropolis virtual world for kids opens, funded by Nickelodeon.

2006

2007

Three Rings Design opens its Whirled virtual world for beta testing.

Ogoglio, a 3D web/virtual world platform, is announced.

HiPiHi, a Chinese-developed virtual world platform opens for beta testing.

Halting State, Charles Stross's MMORPG/AR novel, is published.

Metaplace, Ralph Koster's virtual world platform, is announced.

Apple launches the iPhone. Google makes public its Android open-source software operating system for mobile.

Vast Park opens, an Australian-based virtual world and architectural collaboration platform.

OpenSimulator project goes alpha, running on the OpenSim technology.

The Austrian hybrid virtual world Papermint, a 3D virtual world with "flat" paper cutout characters, enters public beta.

The New Zealand SmallWorlds virtual world opens, an in-browser virtual world similar to Habbo Hotel.

2008

Hello Kitty Online enters beta, based on the famous cartoon characters produced by the Japanese company Sanrio.

Wikitude AR browser launches on the Android platform. Layar Reality Browser launches on the iPhone platform.

Foursquare, a location-based social networking game, is created by Dennis Crowley and Naveen Selvadura.

Avatar, the science-fiction epic directed by James Cameron, becomes the top-grossing film of all time in North America.

2009

Glossary

Actual Addresses a shift from a binary of virtual/real places and events to an understanding of networked media as a spectrum of sites in which agency participates with effects across simulated, terrestrial, and embodied terrain; actual suggests an effect across sites of engagement as opposed to within a virtual or real. (See also *X-reality*.)

Agency The possibility of self-determinant action; how a subject understands him or herself as an actor in an environment, as well as how the subject's effect on such an environment might be gauged, as defined by Albert Bandura's model of emergent interactive agency.

Alternate reality games (ARG) Refers to a fictive or alternate narrative world overlaid on the real world. Often such alternate realities engage multiple media formats, including mobile telephony, websites, and live-action play. ARG is a type of pervasive game play.

Augmented reality A visualization system or other technique that adds an overlay of information onto what can be perceived normally. A browser is used on a mobile device such as a phone or camera to see the augmented artifact (also known as site-specific metadata). The broader definition of augmented reality includes the multiple technical forms we engage to add information, connection, and increase presence in daily life. This includes platforms such as mobile telephony, real-time applications, social

media, and locative media. Embedded in the concept of networked media is the experience of an augmented reality.

Avatar Incarnation of a deity in mortal form, often as a hero (Hindu); a computer-generated figure animated by player or participant in online media context, such as a virtual world; the gestalt of images, text, and multimedia that facilitate presence in networked media.

Behavioral modeling According to experimental psychology, the process by which people are influenced by example.

Copresence The sense of being together with others via mediation.

Embodied agent Low-level, artificial intelligence (AI) program (also known as intelligent agent and software agent) visualized as an animated figure, most often a human one. Embodied agents use technical strategies such as databases of human language, motion and facial expression recognition to respond to human interlocutors. These programs are nicknamed "chatbots" for their role as conversational agents, i.e., robotic or automated conversationalists.

Internet of things Sensor-linked objects (social objects), actions, and capacities tethered to a network; sense-able objects.

Media equation States that human beings cannot distinguish between real and simulated signals; experimental work on media perception developed by Byron Reeves and Clifford Nass.

Mirror world A virtual site that reflects a real one.

Network A system in which nodes are connected to each other by way of links. In a social network, the nodes would be people. In a biological one, the nodes might be proteins linked to form a metabolic network. Network theory describes a set of behaviors to which a variety of systems—technical, natural, or social—adhere. Among the key theorists, physicist Albert-László Barabási has been instrumental in defining the mathematical properties of networks, and sociologist Manuel Castells has helped to develop a theory of networks in regard to society.

Networked media Media platforms that are connected to an informational network, e.g., Internet or cellular towers.

Pervasive media A global culture that engages a spectrum of networked technologies. Platforms include virtual worlds, voice-over-Internet protocol (VoIP), mobile rich-media and texting, and microblogging formats. Implicit to pervasive media engagement is a convergence of multiple or transmedia forms. The term borrows from the language of computer science where pervasive computing, also known as ubiquitous computing, describes a world in which objects, places, and gestures are included on a computational network.

Platform A framework within which systems operate. In this sense, a virtual world, an actual city, and the conditions/context of software all represent types of platforms.

Presence The sense of being somewhere or present to something via mediation.

Real-time Synchronous perception of an activity or thing, as opposed to asynchronous perception. Networked media have begun to conflate the two categories, but one can still make basic distinctions between the two states in terms of the technical affordances of a platform.

Uncanny valley The uncomfortable feeling a viewer may have when seeing a robot or some other mechanically or simulated object that approaches a near human appearance; the term was coined by roboticist Masahiro Mori.

Virtual worlds Immersive text or graphical multiuser virtual spaces that possess unique rules of technical and cultural engagement.

X-reality A continuum of exchanges between virtual and real spaces. Pervasive media use defines a world that is no longer either virtual or real but representative of a diversity of network combinations.

Index